a cook's book
of vegetables

PEAS
BEANS
GREENS

MURDOCH BOOKS

Published by Murdoch Books Pty Limited.
www.murdochbooks.com.au

Murdoch Books Australia
Pier 8/9, 23 Hickson Road
Millers Point NSW 2000
Phone: + 61 (0) 2 8220 2000
Fax: + 61 (0) 2 8220 2558

Murdoch Books UK Limited
Erico House, 6th Floor North
93–99 Upper Richmond Road
Putney, London SW15 2TG
Phone: + 44 (0) 20 8785 5995
Fax: + 44 (0) 20 8785 5985

Chief Executive: Juliet Rogers
Publishing Director: Kay Scarlett

Design Manager: Vivien Valk
Design Concept, Design and Illustration: Alex Frampton
Project Manager: Emma Hutchinson
Editor: Gordana Trifunovic
Introduction text: Leanne Kitchen
Recipes developed by the Murdoch Books Test Kitchen
Production: Maiya Levitch

National Library of Australia Cataloguing-in-Publication Data
Peas, beans and greens: a cook's book of vegetables. Includes index.
ISBN 978 1 74045 761 3. ISBN 1 74045 761 7.
1. Cookery (Vegetables). 641.65

Printed by Midas Printing (Asia) Ltd. in 2006. PRINTED IN CHINA.

IMPORTANT: Those who might be at risk from the effects of salmonella poisoning (the elderly, pregnant women, young children and those suffering from immune deficiency diseases) should consult their doctor with any concerns about eating raw eggs.

CONVERSION GUIDE: You may find cooking times vary depending on the oven you are using. For fan-forced ovens, as a general rule, set the oven temperature to 20°C (35°F) lower than indicated in the recipe. We have used 20 ml (4 teaspoon) tablespoon measures. If you are using a 15 ml (3 teaspoon) tablespoon, for most recipes the difference will not be noticeable. However, for recipes using baking powder, gelatine, bicarbonate of soda (baking soda), small amounts of flour, add an extra teaspoon for each tablespoon specified.

a cook's book
of vegetables

PEAS
BEANS
GREENS

Contents

The green life

'Eat your greens!' is a parent-to-child admonishment that resonates around dining rooms the world over, often accompanied by the threat of 'no pudding' for non-compliance. The reason for what seems a universally early dislike of vegetables is surely in the Great Mystery category as, once we all get a little older and come to our senses, we realize that vegetables comprise some of the most interesting, healthy and utterly delicious foods around. What's not to love, for example, about a heap of scrumptious green peas, glistening with melted, minty, butter; a soothing mass of rich potato mash or a tender cob of corn, bursting with juices, flavour and sweetness? Imagine life without roasted root vegetables, cooked to chewy, mellow perfection and served drenched in meaty gravy, or snappy green leaves bathed in vinegar and oil. Could one manage without the bright, versatile presence of celery, garlic, carrot or onion in sauces, braises, stir-fries, tarts or gratins? Most probably not. Ever since we stopped foraging for food all those aeons ago and began to regulate the vegetable supply by growing things in neat, watered rows, vegetables, in all their glorious forms, have been nurturing our bodies and keeping us in touch with the seasons. The first broad beans to appear, for example, tell us spring is nearly here, while sweet, earthy roots (parsnip, sweet potato, turnip, beets) cheer the winter table with their satisfying tastes and textures. The very essence of summer is found in its crops of zucchini (courgette), eggplant (aubergine), cucumber and lettuce while the slight chill of autumn brings out the best in cauliflower, broccoli and English spinach. Cooking according to seasonal availability has become a modern-day kitchen mantra but one that makes much sense — for fresh goodness and the punchiest flavours it is vital to choose vegetables at their seasonal best. Some are in year-round supply (leeks, beans and cabbage, for example) while others, such as the tomato, make for most satisfying eating when delivered sun-ripened, straight from their vines.

A vegetable dish can be as quick and fuss-free to knock together as boiled globe artichokes splashed with aromatic vinaigrette, stir-fried bok choy (pak choy) or honey-glazed carrots. It might be a classic which never needs updating — like coleslaw or potato cake. Or, a vegetable dish might cause utter surprise, by combining flavours and techniques that never occurred to us (but luckily occurred to someone else!); think deep-fried parmesan carrots or a chargrilled cauliflower salad with sesame dressing. Whatever the occasion or season, vegies offer endless possibilities in the kitchen and deserve to be meal time stars.

Coleslaw Watercress Salad Bok Choy Sala

Leaves and florets

Garden Salad Spinach Salad Chef's Salad

Coleslaw

Serves 4

155 g (5 1/2 oz/2 cups) green cabbage, finely shredded
155 g (5 1/2 oz/2 cups) red cabbage, finely shredded
2 carrots, grated
3 spring onions (scallions), finely chopped
60 g (2 1/4 oz/1/4 cup) mayonnaise
1 tablespoon white wine vinegar
1/2 teaspoon dijon mustard

1 Combine the green and red cabbage, carrot and spring onion in a large bowl and toss together until well combined.

2 Whisk together the mayonnaise, vinegar and mustard. Season with salt and pepper. Pour over the salad and toss to combine.

Baby Spinach Salad

Serves 4

2 tablespoons olive oil
1 tablespoon lemon juice
150 g (5^1/$_2$ oz) baby English spinach leaves
100 g (3^1/$_2$ oz) small black olives

1 Whisk together the olive oil and lemon juice.

2 Put the spinach and olives in a large serving bowl and pour over the dressing. Season with sea salt and freshly ground black pepper. Gently toss to combine.

Roast Broccoli

Serves 4

800 g (1 lb 12 oz) broccoli, cut into florets
1 tablespoon ground cumin
1 tablespoon ground coriander
5 garlic cloves, crushed
2 teaspoons chilli powder
80 ml (2½ fl oz/⅓ cup) oil

1 Preheat the oven to 200°C (400°F/Gas 6). Toss the broccoli with the cumin, coriander, garlic, chilli and oil.

2 Spread the broccoli out on a baking tray and roast for 20 minutes, or until cooked through.

Brussels Sprouts Stir-Fry with Bacon

Serves 4

400 g (14 oz) brussels sprouts, shredded
oil, for cooking
4 bacon slices, finely chopped
chopped almonds, to serve

1   Fry the brussels sprouts in a frying pan with a little oil until tender. Add the bacon and fry together until crisp.

2   To serve, season with pepper and sprinkle a few chopped almonds over the brussels sprouts.

When buying brussels sprouts, choose the smaller ones as they are more tender and tastier, and check they have tight heads and that the leaves are bright green with no tinges of yellow.

Watercress Salad

serves 4–6

500 g (1 lb 2 oz) watercress, picked over
3 celery stalks, cut into 5 cm (2 in) pieces
1 Lebanese (short) cucumber, cut in half, seeded and thinly sliced
3 oranges, cut into segments
1 red onion, thinly sliced and separated into rings
35 g (1¼ oz/¾ cup) snipped chives
60 g (2¼ oz/½ cup) chopped pecans or walnuts

DRESSING
60 ml (2 fl oz/¼ cup) olive oil
60 ml (2 fl oz/¼ cup) lemon juice
2 teaspoons grated orange zest
1 teaspoon wholegrain mustard
1 tablespoon honey

1 Break the watercress into small sprigs, discarding the coarser stems.

2 To make the dressing, combine the ingredients and freshly ground black pepper in a screw-top jar and shake well to combine.

3 Combine all the salad ingredients except the nuts in a large serving bowl. Pour the dressing over and toss to combine. Sprinkle with the chopped pecans or walnuts.

Mixed Green Salad

serves 6–8

3 large cos (romaine) lettuce leaves
4 large butter lettuce leaves
10 red oakleaf lettuce leaves
60 g (2¼ oz) snow pea (mangetout) sprouts, trimmed
1 Lebanese (short) cucumber, cut into thin diagonal slices
250 g (9 oz) cherry tomatoes, cut in half

DRESSING
2 tablespoons lemon juice
60 ml (2 fl oz/¼ cup) olive oil
1 garlic clove, crushed
1 teaspoon soft brown sugar
1 tablespoon finely chopped coriander (cilantro) leaves

1 Tear the lettuce leaves into bite-sized pieces and place in a large serving bowl with the snow pea sprouts, cucumber and tomatoes.

2 To make the dressing, combine the ingredients in a small screw-top jar and shake well. Drizzle the dressing over the salad and toss to combine.

Cauliflower Cheese

Serves 4

500 g (1 lb 2 oz) cauliflower, cut into florets
30 g (1 oz) butter
30 g (1 oz) plain (all-purpose) flour
310 ml (10¾ fl oz/1¼ cups) warm milk
1 teaspoon dijon mustard
60 g (2¼ oz/½ cup) grated cheddar cheese
60 g (2¼ oz/½ cup) grated parmesan cheese
2 tablespoons fresh breadcrumbs
60 g (2¼ oz/½ cup) grated cheddar cheese, extra

1 Brush a 1.5 litre (52 fl oz/6 cup) heatproof dish with melted butter or oil. Cook the cauliflower in lightly salted boiling water until just tender. Drain. Place in the dish and keep warm.

2 Melt the butter in a saucepan. Stir in the flour and cook for 1 minute, or until golden and bubbling. Remove from the heat and whisk in the milk and mustard. Return to the heat and bring to the boil, stirring constantly. Cook, stirring, over low heat for 2 minutes, then remove from the heat. Add the cheeses and stir until melted. Season with salt and white pepper and pour over the cauliflower.

3 Mix together the breadcrumbs and extra cheddar cheese and sprinkle over the sauce. Grill (broil) until the top is browned and bubbling.

Broccoli, Shallots and Chestnuts

Serves 4

200 g (7 oz) small broccoli florets
150 g (5^1/$_2$ oz) fresh chestnuts
60 ml (2 fl oz/^{1}/$_4$ cup) oil
2 thin slices pancetta
2 teaspoons olive oil
3 French shallots, peeled and quartered
1 garlic clove, crushed
1 teaspoon hazelnut oil

1 Boil the broccoli in a large saucepan of boiling salted water for
   4 minutes. Remove with a slotted spoon.

2 Peel and clean the chestnuts. Add to the boiling water and cook
   for 12–15 minutes, or until tender (the chestnuts may break up).
   Drain the chestnuts.

3 Heat the oil in a large frying pan over high heat. Fry the pancetta for
   about 1 minute, or until crisp. Drain on paper towels.

4 Wipe out the pan and heat the olive oil over low heat. Add the
   French shallots and garlic clove. Fry for 5 minutes, or until softened.
   Stir in the chestnuts and cook for 2 minutes. Add the broccoli and
   hazelnut oil and cook until heated through. Break the pancetta
   into shards and add to the pan along with some pepper.

Chef's Salad

Serves 6

1 iceberg lettuce, separated
3 hard-boiled eggs, shelled and chopped
125 g (4^1/$_2$ oz) ham, cut into strips
3 spring onions (scallions), sliced
4 bacon slices, diced
60 ml (2 fl oz/^{1}/$_4$ cup) white wine vinegar
1 teaspoon caster (superfine) sugar
Worcestershire sauce, to taste
2 tablespoons chopped black olives

1 Put the lettuce leaves, egg, ham and spring onions in a salad bowl.

2 Cook the bacon in a frying pan until crisp.

3 Add the vinegar, sugar, Worcestershire sauce and salt and pepper to the lettuce. Crumble the bacon on top, sprinkle with the chopped olives and toss to combine.

Braised Witlof

serves 4

8 witlof (chicory/Belgian endive) heads
20 g (3/4 oz) butter
1 teaspoon soft brown sugar
2 teaspoons tarragon vinegar
100 ml (3 1/2 fl oz) chicken stock
2 tablespoons thick (double/heavy) cream

1 Trim the ends from the witlof. Melt the butter in a deep frying pan
   and fry the witlof briefly on all sides. Add the sugar, vinegar and
   chicken stock and bring to the boil. Reduce the heat to a simmer
   and cover the pan.

2 Simmer gently for 30 minutes, or until tender, turning halfway
   through. Remove the lid from the pan and simmer until nearly all the
   liquid has evaporated. Stir in the cream and serve.

Stuffed Globe Artichokes

Serves 4

40 g (1¹/₂ oz/¹/₄ cup) raw almonds
4 young globe artichokes
1 lemon
150 g (5¹/₂ oz) ricotta cheese
2 garlic cloves, crushed
80 g (2³/₄ oz/1 cup) coarse fresh breadcrumbs
1 teaspoon finely grated lemon zest
50 g (1³/₄ oz/¹/₂ cup) grated parmesan cheese
1 small handful chopped flat-leaf (Italian) parsley
1 tablespoon olive oil
40 g (1¹/₂ oz) butter
2 tablespoons lemon juice

1 Preheat the oven to 180°C (350°F/ Gas 4). Spread the almonds on a baking tray and bake for 5–10 minutes, or until lightly golden. Allow to cool, then remove from the tray and chop.

2 Remove any tough outer leaves from the artichokes. Cut across the artichokes, about 3 cm (1¹/₄ in) from the top, and trim the stalks, leaving about 2 cm (³/₄ in). Rub with lemon and put in a bowl of cold water with a little lemon juice to prevent the artichokes from turning brown.

3 Combine the almonds, ricotta, garlic, breadcrumbs, lemon zest, parmesan and parsley in a bowl and season. Gently separate the artichoke leaves and push the filling in between them.

4 Place the artichokes in a steamer and drizzle with the olive oil. Steam for 25–30 minutes, or until tender. Remove and cook under a hot grill (broiler) for about 5 minutes to brown the filling.

5 Melt the butter in a saucepan, remove from the heat and stir in the lemon juice. Arrange the artichokes on a serving plate, drizzle with the butter sauce and season well.

When buying globe artichokes, choose heavy ones with firm heads and stems, and leaves that are tightly overlapping.

Chinese Broccoli in Oyster Sauce

serves 6

1 kg (2 lb 4 oz) Chinese broccoli (gai larn)
1¹/₂ tablespoons oil
2 spring onions (scallions), finely chopped
1¹/₂ tablespoons grated ginger
3 garlic cloves, finely chopped
60 ml (2 fl oz/¹/₄ cup) oyster sauce
1¹/₂ tablespoons light soy sauce
1 tablespoon Chinese rice wine
1 teaspoon soft brown sugar
1 teaspoon roasted sesame oil
125 ml (4 fl oz/¹/₂ cup) chicken stock
2 teaspoons cornflour (cornstarch)

1 Discard any tough-looking broccoli stems and diagonally cut
the broccoli into 2 cm (³/₄ in) pieces through the stem and leaf.
Blanch the broccoli in a saucepan of boiling water for 2 minutes,
or until the stems and leaves are just tender. Refresh in cold water
and dry thoroughly.

2 Heat a wok over high heat, add the oil and heat until very hot.
Stir-fry the spring onion, ginger and garlic for 10 seconds, or until
fragrant. Add the broccoli and cook until the broccoli is heated
through. Combine the remaining ingredients, add to the wok and stir
until the sauce has thickened, tossing to coat the broccoli.

Creamed Spinach

serves 4-6

1.5 kg (3 lb 5 oz) English spinach
10 g (¼ oz) butter
1 garlic clove, crushed
¼ teaspoon freshly grated nutmeg
80 ml (2½ fl oz/⅓ cup) thick (double/heavy) cream
1 tablespoon grated parmesan cheese

1 Remove the tough ends from the spinach stalks and wash the leaves well. Shake to remove any excess water from the leaves, but do not dry completely.

2 Melt the butter in a large frying pan. Add the crushed garlic and the spinach. Season with nutmeg, salt and pepper, and cook over medium heat until the spinach is just wilted. Remove from the heat and place the spinach in a sieve. Press down well to squeeze out all of the excess moisture. Transfer to a chopping board and, using a mezzaluna or a sharp knife, finely chop the spinach.

3 Pour the cream into the frying pan and heat gently. Add the spinach to the pan and stir until warmed through. Arrange the spinach on a serving dish and sprinkle with the parmesan.

Stir-Fried Cauliflower with Cashew Nuts

serves 4

1 tablespoon vegetable or peanut oil

1 onion, cut into thin wedges

2 garlic cloves, crushed

1 tablespoon Madras curry powder or mild curry powder

2 teaspoons mild curry paste

500 g (1 lb 2 oz) cauliflower, cut into small florets

2 tomatoes, cut into wedges

125 ml (4 fl oz/$1/2$ cup) chicken or vegetable stock

2 teaspoons tomato paste (concentrated purée)

60 g ($2^{1}/4$ oz) thick coconut cream

100 g ($3^{1}/2$ oz/$2/3$ cup) unsalted cashew nuts, roasted and
   roughly chopped

coriander (cilantro) leaves, to garnish

1   Heat a wok over high heat, add the oil and swirl to coat. Add the
    onion and stir-fry for 1–2 minutes, or until golden. Add the garlic,
    curry powder and curry paste and stir-fry for 1 minute. Stir in the
    cauliflower and toss until well coated.

2   Add the tomato, stock, tomato paste and coconut cream and stir-fry
    for 5–6 minutes, or until well combined and the cauliflower is
    cooked. Toss through the nuts just before serving and serve garnished
    with the coriander leaves.

Brussels Sprouts with Pancetta

Serves 4

100 g (3¹/₂ oz) pancetta, thinly sliced
20 g (³/₄ oz) butter
4 French shallots, cut into thick rings
1 tablespoon olive oil
1 garlic clove, crushed
500 g (1 lb 2 oz) young brussels sprouts, thickly sliced

1 Preheat the grill (broiler) to hot. Spread the pancetta on a baking tray lined with foil. Grill (broil) for 1 minute, or until crisp. Set aside to cool.

2 Heat the butter and oil in a large frying pan over medium heat. Add the shallots and garlic and fry for 3–4 minutes, or until just starting to brown. Add the brussels sprouts and season with freshly ground black pepper. Fry, stirring often, for 4–5 minutes, or until partly golden and crisp. Remove from the heat, cover and set aside for 5 minutes.

3 Break the pancetta into large shards. Add to the brussels sprouts and toss lightly. Serve immediately.

Braised Red Cabbage

Serves 4-6

60 g (2¹/4 oz) butter
1 onion, chopped
2 garlic cloves, crushed
900 g (2 lb) red cabbage, sliced
2 green apples, peeled, cored and diced
4 cloves
¹/4 teaspoon freshly grated nutmeg
1 bay leaf
2 juniper berries
1 cinnamon stick
80 ml (2¹/2 fl oz/¹/3 cup) red wine
50 ml (1³/4 fl oz) red wine vinegar
2 tablespoons soft brown sugar
1 tablespoon redcurrant jelly
500 ml (17 fl oz/2 cups) vegetable or chicken stock

1 Preheat the oven to 150°C (300°F/Gas 2). Heat 40 g (1¹/2 oz) of the butter in a large flameproof casserole dish. Add the onion and garlic and cook over medium heat for 5 minutes. Add the cabbage and cook for a further 10 minutes, stirring frequently.

2 Add the apple, cloves, nutmeg, bay leaf, juniper berries and cinnamon stick to the dish. Pour in the red wine and cook for 5 minutes. Add the red wine vinegar, brown sugar, redcurrant jelly and stock. Bring to the boil, then cover and cook in the oven for 2 hours.

3 After 2 hours of cooking check the liquid level — there should be about 125 ml (4 fl oz/¹/₂ cup) left. Stir in the remaining butter, season well, and serve.

 To prevent red cabbage from turning grey, cut it with a stainless steel knife. Choose compact, heavy cabbages with crisp leaves. Discard any damaged outer leaves before use.

Celery Salad

Serves 4

8 Chinese celery or celery stalks
2 tablespoons Chinese rice wine
1 tablespoon light soy sauce
1 tablespoon soft brown sugar
1 tablespoon clear rice vinegar
1 teaspoon roasted sesame oil
1 tablespoon finely chopped ginger

1 Cut the celery into thin slices and blanch in a saucepan of boiling water for 1–2 minutes. Refresh in cold water and dry thoroughly. Arrange the celery on a serving dish.

2 Combine the rice wine with the soy sauce, sugar, rice vinegar, sesame oil and ginger. Blend well and pour over the celery just before serving.

Buy celery with crisp, fresh stems. Celery has a high water content so it should be stored in the crisper drawer of the refrigerator wrapped in plastic. To revive wilted celery, sprinkle it with water and put in the fridge until it becomes crisp again.

Rocket with Pancetta and Gorgonzola

Serves 4

DRESSING
50 g (1³/4 oz) gorgonzola cheese
1/2 garlic clove, crushed
1¹/2 tablespoons olive oil
3 teaspoons white wine vinegar
60 ml (2 fl oz/¹/4 cup) pouring (whipping) cream
1/2 teaspoon chopped tarragon

6 thin slices pancetta
2 large handfuls rocket (arugula)
2 tablespoons pine nuts, roasted

1   To make the dressing, mash the gorgonzola with the garlic in a small
    food processor. With the motor running, gradually add the olive oil,
    then the vinegar. Remove from the processor and stir through the
    cream and tarragon. Season with freshly ground black pepper.

2   Grill (broil) the pancetta under a preheated hot grill (broiler) for
    3–4 minutes, or until crisp. Cool, then break into shards. Put
    the rocket, pine nuts, pancetta and the dressing in a serving bowl
    and toss together.

Cauliflower with Pancetta and Caramelized Onions

Serves 4–6

50 g (1³/4 oz) butter
2 onions, thinly sliced
1 bay leaf
2 garlic cloves, finely chopped
1/4 teaspoon freshly grated nutmeg
40 g (1¹/2 oz/¹/4 cup) pine nuts
2 tablespoons finely chopped flat-leaf (Italian) parsley
6 slices pancetta
500 g (1 lb 2 oz) cauliflower, cut into small florets

1 Melt the butter in a large frying pan over medium heat. Add the onion and bay leaf and season with salt and freshly ground black pepper. Cook, stirring occasionally, for 30 minutes, or until the onion is dark brown and caramelized. Add the garlic, nutmeg and pine nuts and cook for a further 5 minutes, then add the parsley. Remove from the heat.

2 Meanwhile, preheat a grill (broiler) to high and cook the pancetta for 3 minutes on each side, or until crisp and golden. Remove from the heat and allow to cool, then break up into smaller pieces.

3 Line a large steamer with baking paper and punch with holes. Put the cauliflower on top and cover with a lid. Sit the steamer over a saucepan or wok of boiling water and steam for 5–6 minutes, or until tender.

4 Arrange the cauliflower on a serving plate, spoon the onion and pine nut mixture over the top and sprinkle with the pancetta. Serve immediately.

 When buying cauliflower, choose ones that have compact, tight white heads with no blemishes or discoloration.

Garden Salad

serves 4

¹/2 green oakleaf lettuce
150 g (5¹/2 oz) rocket (arugula)
1 small radicchio lettuce
1 green capsicum (pepper), cut into thin strips
grated zest of 1 lemon

DRESSING
1 tablespoon roughly chopped coriander (cilantro) leaves
1¹/2 tablespoons lemon juice
1 teaspoon soft brown sugar
1 tablespoon olive oil
1 garlic clove, crushed (optional)

1   Tear the salad greens into bite-sized pieces. Put in a large serving bowl with the capsicum and lemon zest and toss gently to combine.

2   To make the dressing, combine all the ingredients in a small bowl and whisk until the sugar has dissolved. Just before serving, pour the dressing over the salad and toss well.

Stir-fried Bok Choy

Serves 4

2 tablespoons oil
2 garlic cloves, crushed
3 thin slices ginger, crushed
400 g (14 oz) bok choy (pak choy), cut into 5 cm (2 in) lengths
60 ml (2 fl oz/^{1}/$_4$ cup) chicken stock
1 teaspoon soft brown sugar
salt or light soy sauce, to taste
1 teaspoon roasted sesame oil

1 Heat a wok over high heat, add the oil and heat until very hot. Stir-fry the garlic and ginger for 30 seconds. Add the bok choy and stir-fry until it begins to wilt, then add the stock and sugar and season with the salt or soy sauce. Simmer, covered, for 2 minutes, or until the stems and leaves are tender but still green. Add the sesame oil and serve hot.

Broccoli and Cauliflower Salad

Serves 6

250 g (9 oz) broccoli
250 g (9 oz) cauliflower
40 g (1¹/₂ oz/¹/₃ cup) slivered almonds
60 ml (2 fl oz/¹/₄ cup) ready-made Italian salad dressing
1 tablespoon lemon juice

1 Cut the broccoli and cauliflower into florets and put in a large saucepan of boiling water. Cook for 1 minute, then drain and plunge into iced water. Drain well.

2 Preheat the oven to 180°C (350°F/Gas 4). Spread the almonds onto a baking tray lined with foil and put in the oven for 5 minutes, or until golden brown. Remove from the tray and allow to cool.

3 Put the dressing and lemon juice in a small screw-top jar and shake well. Put the vegetables in a serving bowl and pour over the dressing. Sprinkle the roasted almonds on top.

 When buying broccoli look for firm, tightly closed green heads, with no tinges of yellow.

Cauliflower Bhaji

Serves 4

1 teaspoon cumin seeds
80 ml (2¹/2 fl oz/¹/3 cup) oil
¹/4 teaspoon black mustard seeds
250 g (9 oz) all-purpose potatoes, cut into small cubes
750 g (1 lb 10 oz) cauliflower, cut into florets
¹/2 teaspoon ground cumin
¹/2 teaspoon ground coriander
¹/4 teaspoon ground turmeric
¹/2 teaspoon garam masala
2 garlic cloves, finely chopped
2 green chillies, seeded and finely chopped
5 curry leaves

1 Heat a small frying pan over low heat and dry-roast ¹/4 teaspoon of the cumin seeds until aromatic. Grind the roasted seeds to a fine powder using a mortar and pestle.

2 Heat the oil in a heavy-based saucepan over low heat. Add the mustard seeds and remaining cumin seeds, cover and allow to pop for a couple of seconds. Uncover, add the diced potato and fry for 1 minute, stirring occasionally to prevent the potato from sticking to the pan. Add the cauliflower, all the remaining spices, garlic, chilli and curry leaves and stir until well mixed. Add 60 ml (2 fl oz/¹/4 cup) water and bring to the boil. Cover and simmer for 5–7 minutes, or until the cauliflower is cooked and tender. Season with salt.

Mixed Salad with Warm Brie Dressing

Serves 4

1/2 sourdough baguette
165 ml (5 1/2 fl oz) extra virgin olive oil
6 bacon slices
2 garlic cloves
2 baby cos (romaine) lettuces
90 g (3 1/4 oz) baby English spinach leaves
80 g (2 3/4 oz/1/2 cup) pine nuts, roasted
2 French shallots, finely chopped
1 tablespoon dijon mustard
80 ml (2 1/2 fl oz/1/3 cup) sherry vinegar
300 g (10 1/2 oz) ripe brie cheese, rind removed

1 Preheat the oven to 180°C (350°F/Gas 4). Thinly slice the baguette on the diagonal. Use 2 tablespoons of oil to brush both sides of each slice. Place on a baking tray and bake for 20 minutes, or until golden.

2 Remove the bread from the oven and use one garlic clove, cut in half, to rub the bread slices.

3 Place the bacon on a separate tray and bake for 3–5 minutes, or until crisp. Break the bacon into pieces and allow to cool completely.

4 Remove the outer leaves of the cos lettuces. Put the inner leaves in a large bowl with the spinach. Add the bacon, bread and pine nuts.

5 Pour the remaining olive oil into a frying pan and heat gently. Add the shallots and cook until they soften, then crush the remaining garlic clove and add to the pan. Whisk in the mustard and vinegar, then gently whisk in the chopped brie until it has melted. Remove the dressing from the heat and, while it is still warm, pour over the salad and gently toss.

 Lettuce leaves need to be washed thoroughly and dried very well before use. Either dry them with tea towels (dish towels) or paper towels or use a salad spinner, as any moisture left on the leaves will dilute the dressing. Don't leave lettuce to soak for any length of time as the leaves will absorb water and lose their flavour.

Brussels Sprouts in Mustard Butter

Serves 4

500 g (1 lb 2 oz) brussels sprouts
30 g (1 oz) butter
3 teaspoons wholegrain mustard
2 teaspoons honey

1 Trim the ends and remove any loose leaves from the brussels sprouts. Make a small slit across the base of the stem. Put the sprouts in a large steamer and cover with a lid. Sit the steamer over a saucepan or wok of boiling water and steam for 15 minutes, or until tender. Refresh under cold water to stop the cooking process.

2 Put the butter, mustard and honey in a saucepan over low heat and stir to melt the butter. Add the sprouts and toss until well coated in the butter mixture and heated through. Pile onto a serving plate and serve immediately.

Cauliflower Fritters

Serves 4-6

600 g (1 lb 5 oz) cauliflower
55 g (2 oz/1/2 cup) besan (chickpea flour)
2 teaspoons ground cumin
1 teaspoon ground coriander
1 teaspoon ground turmeric
pinch of cayenne pepper
1/2 teaspoon salt
1 egg, lightly beaten
1 egg yolk
oil, for deep-frying

1 Cut the cauliflower into bite-sized florets. Sift the besan and spices into a bowl, then stir in the salt.

2 To make the batter, lightly whisk the beaten egg, egg yolk and 60 ml (2 fl oz/1/4 cup) water in a bowl. Make a well in the centre of the dry ingredients and pour in the egg mixture, whisking until smooth. Stand for 30 minutes.

3 Fill a deep saucepan one-third full of oil and heat to 180°C (350°F), or until a cube of bread dropped into the oil browns in 15 seconds. Dip the florets into the batter, allowing the excess to drain into the bowl. Deep-fry in batches for 3–4 minutes per batch, or until puffed and browned. Drain, sprinkle with salt and extra cayenne, if desired, and serve hot.

Sautéed Silverbeet

Serves 4–6

1 kg (2 lb 4 oz) silverbeet (Swiss chard)
2 tablespoons olive oil
3 garlic cloves, thinly sliced
extra virgin olive oil, to serve

1 Trim the leaves from the stalks of the silverbeet and rinse them in cold water. Blanch the leaves in a large saucepan of boiling, salted water for 1–2 minutes, or until tender but still firm. Drain well. Lay out on a tea towel (dish towel) or tray to cool. Using your hands, gently wring out the excess water from the leaves.

2 Heat the oil in a heavy-based frying pan and cook the garlic over low heat until just starting to turn golden. Add the silverbeet, season with salt and pepper and cook over medium heat for 3–4 minutes, or until warmed through. Transfer to a serving plate and drizzle with extra virgin olive oil. Serve warm or at room temperature.

 Store silverbeet covered and unwashed in the refrigerator for up to 4 days.

Cabbage with Leek and Mustard Seeds

serves 4–6

1 tablespoon oil
40 g (1¹/₂ oz) unsalted butter
2 teaspoons black mustard seeds
2 leeks, trimmed and thinly sliced
500 g (1 lb 2 oz) cabbage, finely shredded
1 tablespoon lemon juice
100 g (3¹/₂ oz) crème fraîche
2 tablespoons chopped flat-leaf (Italian) parsley

1 Heat the oil and butter together in a deep frying pan. Add the mustard seeds, and cook until they start to pop. Add the leek and cook gently for 5–8 minutes, or until softened. Stir in the cabbage and cook over low heat for 4 minutes, or until it wilts and softens.

2 Season the cabbage well with salt and pepper. Add the lemon juice and crème fraîche, and cook for a further 1 minute. Stir in the parsley and serve immediately.

 Leeks often contain dirt between their layers and need to be washed thoroughly. Trim the roots, remove any coarse outer leaves, then wash in a colander under running water.

Globe Artichokes in Aromatic Vinaigrette

Serves 4

2 tablespoons lemon juice
4 large globe artichokes
2 garlic cloves, crushed
1 teaspoon finely chopped oregano
1/2 teaspoon ground cumin
1/2 teaspoon ground coriander
pinch of dried chilli flakes
3 teaspoons sherry vinegar
60 ml (2 fl oz/1/4 cup) olive oil

1 Add the lemon juice to a large bowl of cold water. Trim the artichokes, cutting off the stalks to within 5 cm (2 in) of the base and removing the tough outer leaves. Cut the top quarter of the leaves from each. Slice each artichoke in half from top to base, or into quarters if large. Remove each small, furry choke with a teaspoon, then put the artichokes in the bowl of acidulated water to prevent them from discolouring while you prepare the rest.

2 Bring a large non-reactive saucepan of water to the boil, add the artichokes and a teaspoon of salt and simmer for 20 minutes, or until tender. The cooking time will depend on the artichoke size. Test by pressing a skewer into the base. If cooked, the artichoke will be soft and give little resistance. Strain, then place the artichokes on their cut side to drain.

3 Combine the garlic, oregano, cumin, coriander and chilli flakes in a bowl. Season, and blend in the vinegar. Beating constantly, slowly pour in the oil to form an emulsion.

4 Arrange the artichokes in rows on a platter. Pour the vinaigrette over the top and allow to cool completely.

 Globe artichokes will keep in the refrigerator for up to 1 week if sprinkled with water and sealed in a plastic bag. Alternatively, store them upright in water, like flowers, for several days.

Water Spinach in Flames

Serves 4

2 tablespoons yellow bean sauce (taucheo)
1 tablespoon fish sauce
2 tablespoons oil
500 g (1 lb 2 oz) water spinach (ong choy), cut into 3 cm (1¼ in) lengths
3 garlic cloves, crushed
4 red Asian shallots, thinly sliced

1 Combine the yellow bean sauce and fish sauce in a small bowl.

2 Heat a wok over high heat, add the oil and swirl to coat. Stir-fry the water spinach for 1 minute, or until slightly wilted. Add the garlic and shallots and cook for about 15 seconds. Stir in the sauce and toss for 30 seconds, or until the leaves are well coated and the stems are tender. Serve immediately.

 Water spinach, or ong choy, is an aquatic plant popular in Southeast Asia. It is cooked like spinach and used in soups, curries and stir-fries.

Flash-Cooked Pea Shoots with Garlic

Serves 6

350 g (12 oz) pea shoots
1 teaspoon oil
2 garlic cloves, finely chopped
1¹/₂ tablespoons Chinese rice wine
¹/₄ teaspoon salt

1 Trim the tough stems and wilted leaves from the pea shoots.

2 Heat a wok over high heat, add the oil and heat until very hot. Add the pea shoots and garlic and toss lightly for 20 seconds. Add the rice wine and salt, and stir-fry for 1 minute, or until the shoots are slightly wilted. Transfer to a serving platter, leaving behind most of the liquid. Serve hot, at room temperature, or cold.

 Pea shoots are the delicate leaves at the top of pea plants. If unavailable, spinach or any other leafy green may be substituted.

Cauliflower and Fennel Purée

Serves 6

1 fennel bulb
1 large cauliflower
90 g (3 1/4 oz) butter
1 tablespoon cider vinegar or white wine vinegar
1 teaspoon salt
1/4 teaspoon sugar

1 Reserving the fronds, trim the fennel and finely chop the bulb and thin green stems. Set the stems aside. Cut the cauliflower into florets.

2 In a large saucepan, melt two-thirds of the butter and gently fry the chopped fennel bulb for 5 minutes, stirring occasionally. Add the cauliflower, toss to coat and cook for 1–2 minutes, then add enough water to just cover.

3 Add the vinegar, salt and sugar and bring to the boil. Reduce the heat and simmer for 15 minutes, or until the cauliflower is very tender. Drain thoroughly, then transfer to a food processor and blend to a smooth purée. Stir in the rest of the butter and the chopped fennel stems. Season to taste and garnish with fennel fronds.

Broccoli and Onion Stir-Fry

Serves 4

250 g (9 oz) broccoli
1 onion
2 teaspoons sesame oil
2 teaspoons vegetable oil
2 teaspoons soy sauce
3 teaspoons sweet chilli sauce

1 Cut the broccoli into small florets. Slice the onion into eight wedges.
Heat the sesame oil and the vegetable oil in a frying pan or wok. Add
the broccoli and onion and cook until tender. Stir in the soy sauce
and sweet chilli sauce. Sprinkle with herbs.

Store onions in a cool, dark place but not
in the refrigerator as their strong odour
will permeate other foods.

Braised Celery

Serves 6

30 g (1 oz) butter
1 celery stalk, trimmed and cut into 5 cm (2 in) lengths
500 ml (17 fl oz/2 cups) chicken stock
2 teaspoons finely grated lemon zest
60 ml (2 fl oz/1/4 cup) lemon juice
60 ml (2 fl oz/1/4 cup) pouring (whipping) cream
2 egg yolks
1 tablespoon cornflour (cornstarch)
1 handful chopped flat-leaf (Italian) parsley
1/2 teaspoon ground mace

1 Preheat the oven to 180°C (350°F/Gas 4). Lightly grease a 1.5 litre (52 fl oz/6 cup) shallow heatproof dish.

2 Melt the butter in a large frying pan. Add the celery and toss to coat. Cover and cook for 2 minutes.

3 Pour over the chicken stock, lemon zest and juice. Cover and simmer for 10 minutes. Remove the celery with a slotted spoon and place in the prepared dish. Reserve 60 ml (2 fl oz/1/4 cup) of the cooking liquid.

4 Blend the cream, egg yolks and cornflour. Whisk in the reserved cooking liquid. Return to the heat and cook until the mixture boils and thickens. Add the parsley and mace and season.

5 Pour the sauce over the celery and cook in the oven for 15–20 minutes, or until the celery softens.

Japanese Spinach Salad

Serves 4

2 eggs
1 sheet nori, cut into matchsticks
100 g (3¹/2 oz/2 cups) baby English spinach leaves
1 small red onion, thinly sliced
1/2 small daikon radish, thinly sliced
2 Lebanese (short) cucumbers, sliced
30 g (1 oz) pickled ginger, sliced
1 tablespoon sesame seeds, roasted

DRESSING
80 ml (2¹/2 fl oz/¹/3 cup) light olive oil
1 tablespoon clear rice vinegar
1 tablespoon light soy sauce

1   Preheat the grill (broiler) to high. Lightly beat the eggs in a small bowl, then add 1 tablespoon water and the nori. Season with salt and freshly ground black pepper.

2   Heat and lightly grease a 20 cm (8 in) omelette pan. Pour in the egg mixture to make a thin omelette. When lightly browned underneath, place under the grill to set the top, without colouring. Turn out onto a board and allow to cool. Cut the omelette into thin strips.

3   To make the dressing, put the olive oil, vinegar and soy sauce in a small bowl. Whisk gently to combine.

4   Put the spinach leaves, onion, daikon, cucumber, pickled ginger, roasted sesame seeds and omelette strips in a large serving bowl. Add the dressing and gently toss to combine.

Indian Cauliflower with Mustard Seeds

Serves 4

2 teaspoons yellow mustard seeds

2 teaspoons black mustard seeds

1 teaspoon ground turmeric

1 teaspoon tamarind purée

2–3 tablespoons mustard oil

2 garlic cloves, finely chopped

1/2 onion, finely chopped

600 g (1 lb 5 oz) cauliflower, cut into small florets

3 mild green chillies, seeded and finely chopped

2 teaspoons nigella seeds

1 Grind the mustard seeds together to a fine powder in a spice grinder or mortar and pestle. Mix with the turmeric, tamarind purée and 100 ml (31/2 fl oz) water to form a smooth, quite liquid paste.

2 Heat 2 tablespoons of the oil in a large, heavy-based saucepan over medium heat until almost smoking. Reduce the heat to low, add the garlic and onion and fry until golden. Cook the cauliflower in batches, adding more oil if necessary, and fry until lightly browned. Add the chilli and fry for 1 minute, or until tinged with brown around the edges.

3 Return all the cauliflower to the pan, sprinkle with the mustard mixture and nigella seeds and stir well. Increase the heat to medium and bring to the boil.

4   Reduce the heat to low, cover and cook until the cauliflower is nearly tender and the seasoning is dry. You may have to sprinkle a little more water on the cauliflower as it cooks to stop it sticking to the pan. If there is still excess liquid when the cauliflower is cooked, simmer with the lid off until it dries out. Season with salt to taste, then remove from the heat.

 Cook cauliflower in a non-aluminium saucepan as aluminium reacts with cauliflower and can turn it yellow.

Butter-baked Baby Cabbage

Serves 4

1 baby cabbage (about 500 g/1 lb 2 oz), cut into 4 wedges
2 tablespoons chicken stock
50 g (1³/4 oz) butter
large pinch of ground ginger
large pinch of sweet paprika
4 thyme sprigs

1 Preheat the oven to 180°C (350°F/Gas 4). Put the baby cabbage wedges, cut side up, in a small baking dish. Add the chicken stock.

2 Melt the butter in a small saucepan and stir in the ginger and paprika. Drizzle over the cabbage wedges and place a thyme sprig on each wedge.

3 Bake for 40 minutes, or until tender and slightly crisp around the edges. If not quite cooked, cover with foil and bake for a further 10–15 minutes. Spoon any pan juices over the top to serve.

Purée of Spinach

Serves 4

1 kg (2 lb 4 oz) English spinach leaves
50 g (1³/4 oz) butter, cubed
80 g (2³/4 oz) crème fraîche
¹/2 teaspoon freshly grated nutmeg

1 Wash the spinach and put in a large saucepan with just the water clinging to the leaves. Cover the pan and steam the spinach for 2 minutes, or until just wilted. Drain, allow to cool and squeeze dry using your hands. Finely chop.

2 Put the spinach in a small saucepan and gently heat through. Increase the heat and gradually add the butter, stirring constantly. Add the crème fraîche and stir into the spinach until it is glossy. Season well and stir in the nutmeg.

Cauliflower with Watercress Dressing

Serves 4–6

1/2 large head cauliflower, cut into florets
90 g (3 1/4 oz/3 cups) watercress, picked over
1 large handful flat-leaf (Italian) parsley, roughly chopped
2 garlic cloves, chopped
2 teaspoons lemon juice
125 g (4 1/2 oz/1/2 cup) whole-egg mayonnaise
40 g (1 1/2 oz/1/4 cup) pine nuts, roasted

1   Line a steamer with baking paper and punch with holes. Lay the
    cauliflower florets in a single layer on top and cover with a lid. Sit
    the steamer over a saucepan or wok of boiling water and steam for
    12–15 minutes, or until tender.

2   Meanwhile, blanch the watercress in boiling water. Drain well. Put
    the watercress, parsley, garlic and lemon juice in a food processor
    and blend until roughly chopped. Add the mayonnaise and pulse
    to combine.

3   Arrange the hot cauliflower on a serving dish and drizzle the
    watercress dressing over the top. Garnish with pine nuts and serve
    hot or cold.

Broccoli with Horseradish Sauce

Serves 6

HORSERADISH SAUCE
60 g (2 1/4 oz) butter, melted
185 g (6 1/2 oz/3/4 cup) mayonnaise
2 tablespoons horseradish cream
1 small onion, grated
1/4 teaspoon mustard powder
pinch of paprika

250 g (9 oz) broccoli, cut into florets
1 tablespoon lemon juice
20 g (3/4 oz) butter, extra

1   To make the horseradish sauce, combine the melted butter, mayonnaise, horseradish, onion, mustard and paprika. Season to taste with salt and pepper. Chill.

2   Cook the broccoli in a saucepan of boiling water for 6–8 minutes. Refresh under cold running water. Drain well.

3   Reheat the broccoli with the lemon juice and extra butter and serve with the horseradish sauce.

Fattoush

Serves 4

1 Lebanese (large pitta) bread, split

2 baby cos (romaine) lettuces, torn into bite-sized pieces

2 tomatoes, chopped

2 small Lebanese (short) cucumbers, chopped

1 green capsicum (pepper), cut into large dice

4 spring onions (scallions), chopped

1 large handful mint, roughly chopped

1 large handful coriander (cilantro) leaves, roughly chopped

DRESSING

60 ml (2 fl oz/1/4 cup) lemon juice

60 ml (2 fl oz/1/4 cup) olive oil

1 tablespoon sumac

1 Preheat the oven to 180°C (350°F/Gas 4). Place the Lebanese bread on a baking tray and bake for 5 minutes, or until golden and crisp. Remove from the oven and allow to cool. Break the bread into 2 cm (3/4 in) pieces.

2 To make the dressing, combine the lemon juice, oil and sumac and season to taste.

3 Put the lettuce, tomato, cucumber, capsicum, spring onion and herbs in a serving bowl and toss to combine. Crumble over the toasted bread and drizzle with the dressing.

Bok Choy Salad

Serves 4

250 ml (9 fl oz/1 cup) chicken stock
1 small carrot, cut into julienne strips
4 baby bok choy (pak choy)
100 g (3 1/2 oz) snow peas (mangetout), thinly sliced
90 g (3 1/4 oz/1 cup) bean sprouts, trimmed
1 tablespoon chopped coriander (cilantro) leaves

DRESSING
80 ml (2 1/2 fl oz/1/3 cup) peanut oil
1 teaspoon sesame oil
1 tablespoon white vinegar
1 tablespoon sesame seeds, roasted
2 teaspoons grated ginger
2 teaspoons honey, warmed
1 garlic clove, crushed

1 Pour the chicken stock into a frying pan and bring to the boil. Add the carrot and bok choy, cover and cook for 2 minutes. Drain the vegetables and allow to cool, then halve the bok choy lengthways.

2 To make the dressing, put the oils, vinegar, sesame seeds, ginger, honey and garlic in a small bowl and whisk to combine. Season with salt and pepper, to taste.

3 Put the carrot and bok choy in a large serving dish and arrange the snow peas, bean sprouts and coriander on top. Drizzle with the sesame dressing and serve immediately.

Warm Globe Artichoke Salad

Serves 4

8 young globe artichokes (200 g/7 oz each)
1 lemon
1 large handful shredded basil
50 g (1³/4 oz/¹/2 cup) shaved parmesan cheese

DRESSING
1 garlic clove, finely chopped
¹/2 teaspoon sugar
1 teaspoon dijon mustard
2 teaspoons finely chopped lemon zest
60 ml (2 fl oz/¹/4 cup) lemon juice
80 ml (2¹/2 fl oz/¹/3 cup) extra virgin olive oil

1 Remove the tough outer leaves from the artichokes until you get to the pale green leaves. Cut across the top of the artichoke, halfway down the tough leaves, then trim the stems to 4 cm (1¹/2 in) long, and lightly peel them. Cut each artichoke in half lengthways and remove the hairy choke with a teaspoon. Rub each artichoke with lemon while you work and place in a bowl of cold water mixed with lemon juice to prevent the artichokes from turning brown.

2 Place the artichokes in a large saucepan of boiling water, top with a plate or heatproof bowl to keep them immersed, and cook for 25 minutes, or until tender. To check tenderness, place a skewer into the largest part of the artichoke. It should insert easily. Drain and cut in half again to serve.

3 To make the dressing, mix the garlic, sugar, mustard, lemon zest and lemon juice in a bowl. Season with salt and freshly ground black pepper, then whisk in the oil with a fork until combined. Pour over the artichoke and scatter with the basil and parmesan.

 Always cut globe artichokes with a stainless steel knife to avoid staining the flesh. Cook in stainless steel, glass or enamel pans, as aluminium pans can impart a metallic flavour and will discolour the artichoke.

Curly Endive and Blue Cheese Salad

Serves 6

3 slices bread
60 ml (2 fl oz/^{1}/4 cup) oil
30 g (1 oz) butter
1 head curly endive
125 g (4^1/2 oz) blue cheese
2 tablespoons olive oil
3 teaspoons white wine vinegar
2 tablespoons snipped chives

1 To make croutons, remove the crusts from the bread and cut into small squares. Heat the oil and butter in a frying pan until bubbling and add the bread. Cook, tossing frequently, for 3 minutes or until golden. Drain on paper towels.

2 Put the curly endive leaves in a serving bowl and crumble the blue cheese over the top.

3 Put the oil and vinegar in a small screw-top jar and shake well. Drizzle over the salad, add the chives and croutons and gently toss to combine.

Chinese Broccoli with Soy Sauce

Serves 4

500 g (1 lb 2 oz) Chinese broccoli (gai larn)
2 tablespoons oil
1 tablespoon oyster sauce
2 tablespoons light soy sauce

1 Discard any tough-looking broccoli stems and cut the remaining
stems in half. Blanch the broccoli in a saucepan of boiling water for
2 minutes, or until the stems and leaves are just tender. Refresh in
cold water and dry thoroughly. Arrange in a serving dish.

2 Heat a wok over high heat, add the oil and heat until very hot.
Carefully pour the hot oil over the broccoli. Gently toss the oil
through the broccoli and drizzle with the oyster sauce and
soy sauce. Serve hot.

Chinese broccoli, or gai larn, is distinguished
by its small white flowers. Young stalks are
crisp and mild; thicker stalks need to be
peeled and halved.

Broccoli and Almond Stir-fry

Serves 4

1 teaspoon coriander seeds

60 ml (2 fl oz/¼ cup) olive oil

2 tablespoons slivered almonds

1 garlic clove, crushed

1 teaspoon finely shredded ginger

500 g (1 lb 2 oz) broccoli, cut into small florets

2 tablespoons red wine vinegar

1 tablespoon soy sauce

2 teaspoons sesame oil

1 teaspoon sesame seeds, roasted

1　Lightly crush the coriander seeds using a mortar and pestle.

2　Heat the oil in a wok or a large heavy-based frying pan. Add the coriander seeds and almonds. Stir over medium heat for 1 minute, or until the almonds are golden.

3　Add the garlic, ginger and broccoli to the pan. Stir-fry over high heat for 2 minutes. Remove the pan from the heat. Pour the combined vinegar, soy sauce and oil into the pan. Toss until the broccoli is well coated. Serve immediately, sprinkled with roasted sesame seeds.

 This dish may be prepared up to 2 hours ahead. Cook just before serving.

Brussels Sprouts with Chestnut and Sage Butter

Serves 4

25 g (1 oz) butter, softened
25 g (1 oz) peeled, cooked chestnuts, finely chopped
1 teaspoon chopped sage
700 g (1 lb 9 oz) brussels sprouts

1 Put the butter, chopped chestnuts and sage in a bowl and mix together well. Scrape onto a large piece of baking paper and shape into a log, using the paper to help shape the butter. Wrap in the paper and refrigerate until firm.

2 Cook the brussels sprouts in boiling salted water for 10–12 minutes, or until tender. Drain well. Cut the chilled chestnut butter into thin slices. Toss four of the slices with the sprouts until they are evenly coated in butter, and season well. Arrange the remaining slices on top of the sprouts and serve immediately.

Mediterranean-style Lettuce

Serves 4

12 large cos (romaine) lettuce leaves
80 ml (2^{1}/$_{2}$ fl oz/^{1}/$_{3}$ cup) olive oil
^{1}/$_{2}$ red capsicum (pepper), cut into fine matchsticks
2 spring onions (scallions), cut into 1 cm (^{1}/$_{2}$ in) pieces
1 tablespoon snipped chives
1 tablespoon lemon juice
2 teaspoons crumbled feta cheese
^{1}/$_{4}$ teaspoon cracked black pepper

1 Tear each lettuce leaf into four pieces. Heat the oil in a frying pan and add the capsicum. Stir over low heat for 1 minute.

2 Add the lettuce to the pan. Toss over high heat for 1 minute, or until the leaves are well coated with the oil. Remove the lettuce from the pan. Reduce the heat to low.

3 Add the spring onions, chives and juice to the pan. Cook, covered, for 30 seconds. Remove the pan from the heat.

4 Combine the lettuce and spring onion mixture and place on a serving plate. Sprinkle with the feta and black pepper.

Spinach Salad

serves 2-4

3 slices white bread, crusts removed
150 g (5¹/2 oz) English spinach leaves
2–3 tablespoons pine nuts
3 bacon slices, chopped
8 button mushrooms, thinly sliced
1 small handful basil leaves, shredded
1–2 garlic cloves, crushed
60 ml (2 fl oz/¹/4 cup) olive oil
balsamic vinegar or freshly squeezed lemon juice, to taste

1 Preheat the oven to 190°C (375°F/Gas 5). Cut the bread into small cubes and put on a baking tray. Bake for 10 minutes, or until golden.

2 Tear the spinach leaves into pieces and place in a large serving bowl. Put the pine nuts in a non-stick frying pan and stir gently over low heat until golden brown. Remove and cool slightly. Add the bacon to the pan and cook for 5–6 minutes, or until crispy. Remove and drain on paper towels.

3 Add the pine nuts, bacon, bread cubes, mushrooms and basil to the spinach leaves. Whisk the garlic and oil together and pour over the salad, tossing gently. Drizzle with the vinegar or lemon juice. Sprinkle with salt and freshly ground pepper.

Hot Chilli Cauliflower

Serves 4

400 g (14 oz) cauliflower, cut into small florets
40 g (1¹/₂ oz) butter, melted
1 tablespoon tomato paste (concentrated purée)
2 tablespoons chopped coriander (cilantro)
¹/₄ teaspoon chilli powder

1 Line a steamer with baking paper and punch with holes. Lay the cauliflower florets in a single layer on top and cover with a lid. Sit the steamer over a saucepan or wok of boiling water and steam for 12–15 minutes, or until tender.

2 Combine the remaining ingredients in a bowl and mix well. Toss through the cauliflower. Serve hot.

Broccoli with Cashews

Serves 4

1 tablespoon olive oil
1 garlic clove, crushed
80 g (2³/4 oz/¹/2 cup) cashew nuts
250 g (9 oz) broccoli, cut into small florets

1   Heat the oil in a wok or heavy-based frying pan. Add the garlic and
    cashews. Stir over medium heat for 2 minutes, or until lightly golden.

2   Add the broccoli. Stir-fry for 3–4 minutes, or until just tender.
    Serve hot.

Green Salad with Lemon Vinaigrette

Serves 4

DRESSING

2 teaspoons finely chopped French shallots

1 1/2 teaspoons dijon mustard

pinch of soft brown sugar

3 teaspoons finely chopped basil

1/2 teaspoons grated lemon zest

2 teaspoons lemon juice

3 teaspoons white wine vinegar

3 teaspoons lemon oil or olive oil

2 1/2 teaspoons virgin olive oil

1 baby cos (romaine) lettuce, leaves separated

1 small butter lettuce, leaves separated

30 g (1 oz) watercress leaves, picked over

100 g (3 1/2 oz) rocket (arugula)

1 To make the lemon vinaigrette, whisk the shallot, mustard, sugar, basil, lemon zest, lemon juice and vinegar in a bowl. Mix the lemon oil and virgin olive oil in a small jug and slowly add to the dressing in a thin stream, whisking constantly until smooth and creamy. Season to taste with salt and pepper.

2 Put all the salad greens in a large bowl. Drizzle the dressing over the salad and toss gently to combine.

Cabbage Salad

Serves 6

155 g (5¹/₂ oz) red cabbage, finely shredded
125 g (4¹/₂ oz) green cabbage, finely shredded
2 spring onions (scallions), finely chopped
60 ml (2 fl oz/¹/₄ cup) olive oil
2 teaspoons white wine vinegar
¹/₂ teaspoon dijon mustard
1 teaspoon caraway seeds

1 Combine the red and green cabbage and spring onion in a serving bowl.

2 Put the oil, vinegar, mustard and caraway seeds in a small screw-top jar and shake well.

3 Pour the dressing over the salad and gently toss to combine.

Chargrilled Cauliflower Salad with Sesame Dressing

Serves 4

DRESSING
60 g (2¼ oz) tahini
1 garlic clove, crushed
60 ml (2 fl oz/¼ cup) seasoned rice vinegar
1 tablespoon vegetable oil
1 teaspoon lime juice
¼ teaspoon sesame oil

1 head cauliflower
12 garlic cloves, crushed
2 tablespoons vegetable oil
2 baby cos (romaine) lettuces
50 g (1¾ oz) picked watercress leaves
2 teaspoons sesame seeds, roasted
1 tablespoon finely chopped flat-leaf (Italian) parsley

1   Preheat a chargrill pan or barbecue flat plate to medium heat. To make the dressing, put the tahini, garlic, rice vinegar, vegetable oil, lime juice, sesame oil and 1 tablespoon water in a non-metallic bowl. Whisk until well combined and season to taste.

2   Cut the cauliflower in half, then into 1 cm (½ in) wedges. Put on a baking tray and gently rub with the garlic and vegetable oil. Season well. Chargrill the cauliflower pieces until golden on both sides and cooked through. Remove from the chargrill pan.

3 Arrange the cos leaves and watercress on a serving platter and top with the chargrilled cauliflower slices. Drizzle the tahini dressing over the top and garnish with the sesame seeds and parsley.

 Soak cauliflower in salted water to get rid of any bugs before cooking, then rinse thoroughly.

Spinach and Nut Salad

Serves 4

250 g (9 oz) green beans, trimmed and chopped
90 g (3¹/4 oz) baby English spinach leaves
¹/2 onion, thinly sliced
90 g (3 oz/¹/3 cup) plain yoghurt
1 tablespoon lemon juice
1 tablespoon shredded mint
90 g (2³/4 oz/²/3 cup) chopped walnuts, roasted
mint leaves, to serve

1 Cover the beans with boiling water and leave for 2 minutes. Drain. Pat the beans dry, then allow to cool.

2 Arrange the beans, spinach and onion on a serving plate.

3 Combine the yoghurt, lemon juice and mint in a bowl. Pour over the salad, sprinkle with walnuts and garnish with mint.

 When buying green beans, make sure the pods snap crisply.

Herbed Cabbage

Serves 2

30 g (1 oz) butter
440 g (15¹/₂ oz) cabbage, finely shredded
1 large handful shredded basil

1 Melt the butter in a large saucepan with a lid. Add the cabbage and toss to combine with the butter. Cover and cook the cabbage over low heat for about 5 minutes, or until tender.

2 Remove the lid and lift the cabbage with tongs occasionally to cook evenly. Stir through the basil. Season to taste with salt and freshly ground black pepper and serve immediately.

Warm Radicchio Salad with Crushed Tomato Vinaigrette

Serves 4

100 ml (3½ fl oz) oil
6 garlic cloves, thinly sliced
7 roma (plum) tomatoes, cored and halved
60 ml (2 fl oz/¼ cup) extra virgin olive oil
2 tablespoons red wine vinegar
1 teaspoon honey
900 g (2 lb) witlof (chicory/Belgian endive)
1 onion, cut in half and sliced
1 radicchio lettuce

1. Heat 60 ml (2 fl oz/¼ cup) of the olive oil in a small frying pan. Add the garlic and fry over high heat for a 1–2 minutes, or until lightly browned. Drain on paper towels.

2. Heat 1 tablespoon of the olive oil in a frying pan and cook the tomato, cut side down, over medium heat until browned and very soft. Turn to brown the other side. Transfer to a bowl to cool. Peel and discard the skins. Roughly mash the flesh with a fork.

3. To make the vinaigrette, whisk together about half of the crushed tomatoes and the extra virgin olive oil, vinegar and honey. Season with salt and freshly ground black pepper.

4 Trim the coarse stems from the witlof and cut into short lengths. Heat the remaining olive oil in the frying pan. Add the onion and cook until transparent. Add the witlof and stir until just wilted. Add the remaining tomato and stir until well combined. Season.

5 Tear any large radicchio leaves into smaller pieces. Toss through the witlof mixture. Transfer to a large serving bowl, drizzle with the tomato vinaigrette and sprinkle with the garlic.

 Store witlof in a paper bag in the refrigerator.

Warm Choy Sum Salad

Serves 4

370 g (13 oz) choy sum
2 tablespoons peanut oil
3 teaspoons finely grated ginger
2 garlic cloves, finely chopped
2 teaspoons soft brown sugar
2 teaspoons sesame oil
2 tablespoons soy sauce
1 tablespoon lemon juice
2 teaspoons seasame seeds, roasted

1 Trim the ends from the choy sum and slice in half. Steam for
2 minutes, or until wilted, then arrange on a serving plate.

2 Heat a small saucepan over high heat, add the peanut oil and swirl
to coat the pan. Add the ginger and garlic and stir-fry for 1 minute.
Add the sugar, sesame oil, soy sauce and lemon juice. Heat until hot
and pour over the choy sum. Season to taste with salt and pepper
and garnish with the sesame seeds.

 Choy sum is also known as Chinese
flowering cabbage. It has mild mustard-
flavoured leaves and small yellow flowers.

Asian-style Coleslaw

Serves 4

200 g (7 oz/2²/₃ cups) finely shredded red cabbage
175 g (6 oz/2¹/₃ cups) finely shredded Chinese cabbage (wong bok)
1 large carrot, shredded
1 small red onion, thinly sliced
1 red chilli, seeded and thinly sliced lengthways (optional)
80 g (2³/₄ oz/³/₄ cup) snow peas (mangetout), thinly sliced
1 small handful torn Thai (holy) basil
50 g (1³/₄ oz/¹/₃ cup) roughly chopped roasted peanuts

DRESSING
2 tablespoons lime juice
1¹/₂ teaspoons finely grated ginger
90 g (3¹/₄ oz/¹/₃ cup) light sour cream
1 teaspoon fish sauce
1 garlic clove, crushed

1 Combine the red cabbage and Chinese cabbage in a large bowl. Add the carrot, onion, chilli, snow peas, Thai basil and 2 tablespoons of the peanuts and toss to combine.

2 To make the dressing, put all the ingredients in a small bowl and whisk until combined. Pour over the cabbage mixture and toss to combine. Scatter the remaining peanuts on top. Serve at room temperature.

Spinach and Avocado Salad with Warm Mustard Vinaigrette

Serves 8

90 g (3¼ oz) English spinach leaves

1 red or green curly-leafed lettuce

2 avocados

60 ml (2 fl oz/¼ cup) olive oil

2 teaspoons sesame seeds

1 tablespoon lemon juice

2 teaspoons wholegrain mustard

1   Tear the spinach and lettuce leaves into bite-size pieces. Put in a large serving bowl.

2   Peel the avocados and cut into thin slices. Scatter over the leaves. Heat 1 tablespoon of the oil in a small frying pan. Add the sesame seeds and cook over low heat until they just start to turn golden. Remove from the heat immediately and allow to cool slightly.

3   Add the lemon juice, remaining oil and mustard to the pan and stir to combine. While still warm, pour over the salad and gently toss.

 Cut avocado turns brown, so cut it just before use or brush it with lemon juice to prevent discolouration. Firm, unripe avocados will ripen at room temperature after 3–4 days.

Stir-fried Chinese Cabbage

Serves 4

1 tablespoon oil
400 g (14 oz) Chinese cabbage (wong bok), cut into 1 cm (1/2 in) strips
1 tablespoon light soy sauce
2 teaspoons soft brown sugar
1 tablespoon clear rice vinegar
2 teaspoons roasted sesame oil

1 Heat a wok over high heat, add the oil and heat until very hot. Add the Chinese cabbage and cook for 2 minutes, or until wilted.

2 Add the soy sauce, sugar and rice vinegar and cook for 1 minute. Sprinkle with the sesame oil and serve immediately.

French Peas Snow Pea Salad Minted Peas

Peas and beans

Herbed Green Beans Glazed Peas Green Bean

French Peas

Serves 6

310 g (11 oz/2 cups) peas
75 g (2¹/₂ oz/1 cup) shredded lettuce
60 g (2¹/₄ oz/¹/₂ cup) chopped spring onions (scallions)
2 mint sprigs
¹/₂ teaspoon salt
¹/₄ teaspoon soft brown sugar
60 g (2¹/₄ oz) butter

1 Put the peas, lettuce, spring onion, mint, sugar, and 125 ml
(4 fl oz/¹/₂ cup) water in a saucepan with half of the butter. Season
with salt and freshly ground pepper. Cover and cook over medium
heat for 15 minutes.

2 Remove the mint and add the remaining butter. Gently toss to
combine and serve immediately.

Green Bean and Pine Nut Salad

Serves 4

280 g (10 oz) green beans, trimmed
1 tablespoon olive oil
2 teaspoons lemon juice
1 tablespoon pine nuts, roasted
80 ml (2½ fl oz/⅓ cup) tomato juice
1 garlic clove, crushed
2–3 drops Tabasco sauce

1 Put the beans in a saucepan of boiling water. Boil for 1 minute, then drain and plunge into iced water. Drain again, then toss with the oil and lemon juice.

2 Combine the tomato juice, garlic and Tabasco in a small saucepan and bring to the boil over medium heat. Simmer, uncovered, over low heat for 8 minutes, or until reduced by half. Allow to cool.

3 Arrange the beans on a serving plate and pour over the tomato mixture. Sprinkle with the pine nuts.

Broad Bean Purée

Serves 4

500 g (1 lb 2 oz) fresh or frozen broad (fava) beans
80 ml (2$^{1}/_{2}$ fl oz/$^{1}/_{3}$ cup) olive oil

1 Put the beans in a saucepan and cover with cold water. Bring to the boil and simmer until tender.

2 Mash the beans with the olive oil and enough cooking water to make a spreadable paste. Season well.

Glazed Peas

Serves 4

60 g (2¼ oz) butter
500 g (1 lb 2 oz) peas
1 large lettuce heart, shredded
1 tablespoon flat-leaf (Italian) parsley, chopped
½ teaspoon salt
125 ml (4 fl oz/½ cup) dry white wine

1 Melt the butter in a saucepan over low heat. Add the peas and cook gently until tender. Add the lettuce, parsley and salt.

2 Pour in the wine. Increase the heat and allow the liquid to reduce to half. Serve immediately.

 When buying peas, look for bright, shiny, green pods that feel firm and taut.

Green and Yellow Bean Salad

Serves 6

250 g (9 oz) green beans, trimmed
250 g (9 oz) yellow beans, trimmed
60 ml (2 fl oz/¼ cup) olive oil
1 tablespoon lemon juice
1 garlic clove, crushed
shaved parmesan cheese, to serve

1 Bring a saucepan of lightly salted water to the boil. Add the green and yellow beans and cook for 2 minutes, or until just tender. Plunge into cold water and drain.

2 Put the olive oil, lemon juice and garlic in a bowl, season with salt and freshly ground black pepper, and mix together. Place the beans in a serving bowl, pour the dressing over and toss to coat. Top with the shaved parmesan cheese.

 Yellow beans, also known as wax beans, are like a soft, golden version of string or green beans with a lighter, sweeter taste. Choose fresh, brightly coloured pods that snap when bent in half and avoid any that are spotted, leathery or discoloured. Store fresh beans in an airtight container in the refrigerator for up to 4 days.

Garlic and Basil Beans

Serves 4

1 tablespoon olive oil
1 garlic clove, crushed
20 green beans, trimmed
1 tablespoon shredded basil

1 Heat the olive oil in frying pan or wok over medium heat. Add the garlic and green beans.

2 Cook, stirring, 2–3 minutes or until beans are just tender. Stir in the basil leaves. Serve hot.

Bean and Vegetable Salad with Chilli and Black Vinegar Dressing

Serves 4

2 fennel bulbs, trimmed and sliced lengthways

125 g (4^1/2 oz/^{2}/3 cup) baby corn, cut in half on the diagonal

150 g (5^1/2 oz) snow peas (mangetout), trimmed and cut in half on the diagonal

400 g (14 oz) tinned borlotti (cranberry) beans, drained and rinsed

100 g (3^1/2 oz) baby rocket (arugula)

40 g (1^1/2 oz) snow pea (mangetout) sprouts, trimmed

DRESSING

80 ml (2^1/2 fl oz/^{1}/3 cup) olive oil

60 ml (2 fl oz/^{1}/4 cup) black vinegar

1 tablespoon rice vinegar

2 tablespoons finely chopped coriander (cilantro) leaves

1 small red chilli, seeded and finely chopped

1   Line a steamer with baking paper and punch the paper with holes. Put the fennel and baby corn in the steamer and cover with a lid. Sit the steamer over a saucepan or wok of boiling water and steam for 5 minutes. Add the snow peas and beans and steam for a further 5 minutes. Transfer to a bowl, making sure you leave any condensed steaming liquid on the baking paper.

2   To make the dressing, whisk together the oil, black vinegar and rice vinegar until well combined. Season well with salt and pepper. Stir in the coriander and chilli.

3 Pour half the dressing over the vegetables, toss well, then stand for 5 minutes. Arrange the rocket leaves on a serving platter and drizzle with the remaining dressing. Spoon on the dressed vegetables and scatter the snow pea sprouts over the top.

 Snow peas (mangetout) have a flat thin pod and are best when perfectly fresh; they are not really designed to be stored at all. Left to linger in the fridge, they will quickly wilt, so for best results, buy them on the day you plan to use them. Trim them before cooking.

Beans with Sesame Miso Dressing

Serves 4–6

250 g (9 oz) green beans, trimmed and cut into 5 cm (2 in) lengths

DRESSING
50 g (1³/₄ oz/¹/₃ cup) sesame seeds
1 teaspoon soft brown sugar
2 tablespoons red or white miso paste
2 tablespoons mirin

1 Bring a saucepan of lightly salted water to the boil. Add the beans and cook for 2 minutes, or until just tender. Drain, plunge into iced water until cool, then drain well.

2 To make the dressing, dry-fry the sesame seeds in a frying pan over medium heat, stirring, for 5 minutes, or until lightly golden and aromatic. Grind the sesame seeds in a mortar and pestle, reserving 1 teaspoon of whole seeds for garnish, until finely crushed. Gradually incorporate the sugar, miso and mirin until it forms a thickish paste.

3 Put the beans in a bowl with the dressing and toss to combine. Sprinkle with the reserved sesame seeds.

Warm Bean Salad

Serves 4

2 tablespoons olive oil
1 onion, finely chopped
1 garlic clove, crushed
1 small red capsicum (pepper), cut into small strips
90 g (3$^{1}/_4$ oz) green beans
60 g (2$^{1}/_4$ oz) button mushrooms, sliced
1 tablespoon balsamic vinegar
440 g (15$^{1}/_2$ oz) tinned mixed beans, rinsed and drained
chopped flat-leaf (Italian) parsley, to serve

1   Heat 1 tablespoon of the oil in a frying pan. Add the onions and
    cook for 2 minutes over medium heat. Add the garlic, capsicum,
    green beans, mushrooms and vinegar. Cook for a further 5 minutes,
    stirring occasionally.

2   Add the mixed beans to the vegetables with the remaining oil and
    stir until just warmed through. Sprinkle with the chopped parsley.

Peppered Peas and Garlic

Serves 4

1 tablespoon oil
2 garlic cloves, crushed
1 teaspoon cracked black pepper
310 g (11 oz/2 cups) frozen green peas
1/2 teaspoon sugar
balsamic vinegar, to drizzle (optional)

1   Heat the oil in heavy-based frying pan. Add the garlic and pepper. Stir in the peas and sugar. Cook over medium heat for 2–3 minutes, or until the peas are tender.

2   Drizzle with the balsamic vinegar, if desired. Serve immediately.

 When buying garlic, choose fresh, plump-looking bulbs with a white skin; store in a cool, open place.

Green Beans in a Zesty Sauce

Serves 4

500 g (1 lb 2 oz) green beans, trimmed and cut into 5 cm (2 in) lengths
20 g (³/4 oz) butter
1 teaspoon Worcestershire sauce
1 teaspoon lemon juice
shredded lemon zest, to garnish

1 Bring a saucepan of lightly salted water to the boil. Add the beans
   and cook for 10–12 minutes. Refresh under cold running water,
   then drain well.

2 Melt the butter in a frying pan, then add the sauce, lemon juice and
   drained beans. Stir until well coated and heated through. Season to
   taste. Serve garnished with the lemon zest.

Minted Peas

Serves 4

620 g (1 lb 6 oz/4 cups) fresh or frozen peas
4 mint sprigs
30 g (1 oz) butter
2 tablespoons shredded mint

1 Place the peas in a saucepan and pour in enough water to just cover the peas. Add the mint sprigs.

2 Bring to the boil and simmer for 5 minutes (only 2 minutes if frozen), or until the peas are just tender. Drain and discard the mint sprigs. Return to the saucepan, add the butter and shredded mint and stir over low heat until the butter has melted. Season with salt and pepper.

Buy fresh mint leaves and store for up to 1 week in the refrigerator, or tightly seal in a bag and freeze.

Herbed Green Beans

serves 6

125 g (4^1/$_2$ oz) butter, softened
^{1}/$_2$ teaspoon marjoram, chopped
^{1}/$_2$ teaspoon dried basil, chopped
1 teaspoon chopped flat-leaf (Italian) parsley
1 teaspoon snipped chives
500 g (1 lb 2 oz) green beans, trimmed
1 small onion, chopped
1 garlic clove, crushed
30 g (1 oz/^{1}/$_4$ cup) sunflower seeds

1 Mix the butter with the marjoram, basil, parsley and chives. Place the beans into a large saucepan with the onion and garlic and cover with boiling salted water. Cook over medium heat until tender. Drain well.

2 Add the herb butter to the pan and stir until beans are well coated. Season to taste and add the sunflower seeds just before serving.

Parcels of Snake Beans with Spiced Peanuts

Serves 6

SPICED PEANUTS
80 g (2³/4 oz/¹/2 cup) roasted peanuts
1 garlic clove, finely chopped
1 tablespoon grated ginger
¹/2 teaspoon ground fennel
1 large red chilli, seeded and finely chopped
1 tablespoon grated palm sugar or soft brown sugar
1 tablespoon peanut oil
1 tablespoon lime juice
60 g (2¹/4 oz) fried shallots
2 tablespoons finely chopped coriander (cilantro) leaves

320 g (11¹/4 oz) snake (yard-long) beans, cut into 8 cm (3¹/4 in) lengths
2 teaspoons sesame oil
12 garlic chives

1 Put the peanuts, garlic, ginger, ground fennel, chopped chilli, palm sugar and ¹/2 teaspoon of salt in a food processor. Process until it reaches a coarse texture.

2 Heat the oil in a frying pan over medium–high heat. Add the peanut mixture and cook, stirring well, for 2–3 minutes, or until lightly brown and fragrant. Add the lime juice and fried shallots and cook for a further minute. Remove from the heat and set aside to cool. When the mixture has cooled slightly, toss in the chopped coriander.

3 Meanwhile, put the snake beans in a steamer and cover with a lid. Sit the steamer over a wok or saucepan of boiling water and steam for 5 minutes, or until the beans are tender, then remove and set aside to cool slightly. When the beans are cool enough to handle, toss with the sesame oil.

4 Bundle the beans into 12 even-sized parcels and tie together with a garlic chive. Place the beans on a serving platter and spoon the spiced peanuts over the top. Serve immediately.

Peas with Onions and Lettuce

Serves 6

50 g (1³/4 oz) butter

16 baby onions or French shallots

500 g (1 lb 2 oz) peas

250 g (9 oz) iceberg lettuce heart, finely shredded

2 parsley sprigs

1 teaspoon caster (superfine) sugar

125 ml (4 fl oz/¹/2 cup) chicken stock

1 tablespoon plain (all-purpose) flour

1 Melt 30 g (1 oz) of the butter in a large saucepan. Add the onions and cook, stirring, for 1 minute. Add the peas, shredded lettuce, parsley sprigs and sugar.

2 Pour in the stock and stir well. Cover the pan and cook over low heat for 15 minutes, stirring occasionally, or until the onions are cooked through. Remove the parsley.

3 Mix the remaining butter with the flour. Add small amounts to the vegetables, stirring until the juices thicken slightly. Season with salt and freshly ground black pepper.

Green Beans with Feta and Tomatoes

Serves 4

1 tablespoon olive oil
1 onion, chopped
2 garlic cloves, crushed
1 1/2 tablespoons chopped oregano
125 ml (4 fl oz/1/2 cup) dry white wine
425 g (15 oz) tinned diced tomatoes
250 g (9 oz) green beans, trimmed
1 tablespoon balsamic vinegar
200 g (7 oz) feta cheese, cut into 1.5 cm (5/8 in) cubes

1   Heat the oil in a saucepan, add the onion and cook over medium
    heat for 3–5 minutes, or until soft. Add the garlic and half the
    oregano, and cook for a further minute. Pour in the white wine
    and cook for 3 minutes, or until reduced by one-third.

2   Stir in the diced tomato and cook, uncovered, for 10 minutes. Add
    the beans and cook, covered, for a further 10 minutes.

3   Stir in the balsamic vinegar, feta and remaining oregano. Season
    with salt and freshly ground black pepper.

Snake Beans and Almonds with Green Peppercorn Dressing

Serves 4

250 g (9 oz) snake (yard-long) beans, cut into 10 cm (4 in) lengths
85 g (3 oz/½ cup) blanched almonds

GREEN PEPPERCORN DRESSING
1 tablespoon pickled green peppercorns, drained and coarsely ground
1 tablespoon olive oil
1 tablespoon almond oil
1 tablespoon lemon juice
1 tablespoon dijon mustard

1   Cook the beans in boiling salted water for 2–4 minutes, or until just tender. Drain and put in a serving dish.

2   Dry-fry the almonds in a small frying pan over medium heat for 2–4 minutes. Add to the beans.

3   Combine the dressing ingredients in a small bowl and whisk. Season with salt to taste. Pour the mixture over the beans and toss well. Serve hot or cold.

Sautéed Peas and Spring Onions

Serves 4

30 g (1 oz) butter
310 g (11 oz/2 cups) frozen peas
1 garlic clove, crushed
2 spring onions (scallions), thinly sliced

1   Melt the butter in a heavy-based frying pan. Add the peas, garlic and spring onion. Stir over medium heat for 2–3 minutes, or until the peas and onion are just tender. Serve hot.

 Spring onions are normally sold in bunches — look for ones that have firm white bases and undamaged green tops. The thinner onions will have a milder flavour. Store wrapped in plastic in the refrigerator.

Snow Pea Salad with Japanese Dressing

Serves 4

200 g (7 oz) snow peas (mangetout), trimmed
50 g (1¾ oz) snow pea (mangetout) sprouts, trimmed
1 small red capsicum (pepper), julienned
2 teaspoons sesame seeds, roasted

DRESSING
½ teaspoon dashi granules
1 tablespoon soy sauce
1 tablespoon mirin
1 teaspoon soft brown sugar
1 garlic clove, crushed
1 teaspoon finely chopped ginger
¼ teaspoon sesame oil
1 tablespoon vegetable oil
2 teaspoon sesame seeds, roasted

1. Bring a saucepan of water to the boil, add the snow peas and blanch for 1 minute. Drain and refresh under cold water, then drain again. Toss in a serving bowl with the snow pea sprouts and capsicum.

2. To make the dressing, dissolve the dashi granules in 1½ tablespoons of hot water. Pour into a small bowl, add the remaining dressing ingredients and whisk well. Pour the dressing over the snow peas, toss well and season to taste. Sprinkle with the sesame seeds and serve.

Sautéed Baby Beans with Artichokes and Olives

Serves 4

200 g (7 oz) baby green beans
8 spring onions (scallions)
1 tablespoon olive oil
6 rosemary sprigs
85 g (3 oz/^{1}/$_2$ cup) green olives
2 quartered artichoke hearts in brine
1 tablespoon salted baby capers, rinsed and drained
1 tablespoon extra virgin olive oil
2 teaspoons tarragon vinegar

1 Blanch the baby beans in boiling salted water for 2 minutes, then drain well. Trim the spring onions (scallions) to roughly the same length as the beans.

2 Heat the olive oil in a large frying pan over medium heat. Add the beans, spring onion and rosemary sprigs and cook for 1–2 minutes, or until lightly browned. Remove from the heat.

3 Add the olives, artichokes, capers, extra virgin olive oil and tarragon vinegar. Season with salt and freshly ground black pepper and toss to coat. Transfer to a serving dish and serve warm.

Green Beans with Satay Dressing

Serves 4-6

250 g (9 oz) green beans, trimmed

DRESSING
40 g (1$^{1}/_{2}$ oz/$^{1}/_{4}$ cup) roasted salted peanuts
1 tablespoon sugar
2 tablespoons light soy sauce
1–2 tablespoons chicken stock

1   Put the beans in a saucepan of boiling water and cook for
    10–12 minutes. Refresh under cold running water. Drain well
    and pat dry on paper towels. Cut the beans diagonally into long
    thin slices, cover and refrigerate until required.

2   To make the dressing, finely grind the peanuts in a food processor,
    then add sugar and soy sauce and enough stock to produce a
    spooning consistency. Coat the beans with the dressing.

Sweet Coriander Peas

Serves 4

30 g (1 oz) butter
1½ teaspoons lemon juice
½ teaspoon sugar
310 g (11 oz/2 cups) frozen peas
2 tablespoons finely chopped coriander (cilantro) leaves

1 Heat the butter in a saucepan. Add the lemon juice, sugar and peas. Cook over medium heat for 2–3 minutes, or until just tender. Add the coriander and toss well to combine.

Snow Pea Salad

Serves 4

GARLIC CROUTONS
1¹/2 slices thick white bread, crusts removed
60 ml (2 fl oz/¹/4 cup) olive oil
1 small garlic clove, crushed

DRESSING
1 tablespoon olive oil
2 teaspoons mayonnaise
2 teaspoons sour cream
1 tablespoon lemon juice
¹/2 teaspoon soft brown sugar

100 g (3¹/2 oz) snow peas (mangetout), trimmed and sliced diagonally
¹/2 red capsicum (pepper), sliced
125 g (4¹/4 oz) cherry tomatoes
30 g (1 oz) watercress sprigs, picked over
2 oakleaf lettuce leaves, torn
2 green coral lettuce leaves, torn
shaved parmesan cheese, to serve

1   To make the garlic croutons, cut the bread into 1 cm (¹/2 in) cubes. Heat the oil in a small, heavy-based frying pan and add the garlic. Stir in the bread cubes and cook over medium heat for 4–5 minutes, or until golden and crisp. Remove from the pan and allow to drain on crumpled paper towels.

2 Put the dressing ingredients in a small bowl with cracked black pepper and whisk for 2 minutes, or until well combined.

3 Combine the snow peas, capsicum, tomatoes, watercress and lettuce. Scatter the parmesan over the top. Just before serving, drizzle the dressing over the salad and scatter with the croutons.

Steamed Mixed Bean Bundles

Serves 4

8 long chives
20 green beans, trimmed
20 butterbeans (lima beans), trimmed

1 Place the chives in a small bowl, cover with boiling water to soften, then drain well.

2 Divide the beans into eight bundles and tie them together with a chive. Place the bundles in a steamer over a saucepan half-filled with simmering water. Cover with a lid and steam the beans over medium heat for 5–8 minutes, or until just tender.

3 Sprinkle the cooked beans with salt and freshly ground black pepper and serve immediately.

 Chives are best used when fresh, but can be stored in the vegetable crisper in the refrigerator for up to 2 days.

Three-Bean Salad

Serves 4

100 g (3^1/2 oz) green beans, trimmed and cut into
    4 cm (1^1/2 in) lengths
200 g (7 oz) frozen broad (fava) beans, defrosted
310 g (10^1/2 oz) tinned butterbeans (lima beans), rinsed and drained
310 g (10^1/2 oz) tinned red kidney beans, rinsed and drained
1 small red onion, thinly sliced
2 tablespoons chopped flat-leaf (Italian) parsley
2 tablespoons ready-made French salad dressing

1 Bring a small saucepan of lightly salted water to the boil. Add the green beans and broad beans. Stand for 1 minute over the heat, then drain. Refresh under cold water, then drain again.

2 Place the green beans and broad beans in a serving bowl with all the tinned beans, onion and parsley. Pour the dressing over and toss well.

Wax Beans with Sun-Dried Tomatoes and Capers

Serves 4

2 sun-dried tomatoes in oil, drained, plus 1 teaspoon of the oil

2 teaspoons capers, rinsed and drained

250 g (9 oz) young wax beans, tailed

1 teaspoon light olive oil

zest of 1 lemon, cut into thin strips

1 Slice the sun-dried tomatoes into long, thin strips. Heat the oil from the sun-dried tomatoes in a small frying pan over medium heat. Fry the capers, stirring often, for 1 minute, or until darkened and crisp. Drain on paper towels.

2 Bring a saucepan of water to the boil. Add a large pinch of salt and the wax beans and simmer for 3–4 minutes, or until just tender. Drain, season with freshly ground black pepper and toss with the sun-dried tomatoes, capers, olive oil and lemon zest. Serve hot or at room temperature.

Tempura Snow Peas

Serves 4

1 egg
100 g (3¹/2 oz/³/4 cup) plain (all-purpose) flour, plus extra for coating
vegetable oil, for frying
150 g (5¹/2 oz) young snow peas (mangetout)
ponzu soy sauce, pickled ginger and wasabi paste, to serve

1   Put the egg in a bowl and use chopsticks to lightly break it up. Add
    the flour, 185 ml (6 fl oz/³/4 cup) iced water and salt and freshly
    ground black pepper. Stir with the chopsticks to combine.

2   Fill a wok or heavy-based saucepan one-third full of vegetable oil
    and heat to 180°C (350°F), or when a cube of bread dropped into
    the oil browns in 15 seconds.

3   Lightly coat the snow peas in the extra flour. Working in batches,
    hold the snow peas by their tails and dip them into the batter. Shake
    off the excess and carefully drop the snow peas into the hot oil. Cook
    for 45–60 seconds, or until golden. Drain on paper towels. Serve hot,
    accompanied by small bowls of ponzu soy sauce, pickled ginger and
    wasabi paste.

Mushy Peas with Fennel and Spring Onions

Serves 4

20 g (3/4 oz) butter
1 tablespoon oil
1 baby fennel bulb, thinly sliced
320 g (11 1/4 oz/2 cups) fresh or frozen peas
1 small potato, cut into 2 cm (3/4 in) cubes
250 ml (9 fl oz/1 cup) milk
4 spring onions (scallions), thinly sliced
1 small handful chopped fennel leaves
extra virgin olive oil, for drizzling

1 Heat the butter and oil in a large saucepan over medium–low heat and fry the fennel for 3–4 minutes, or until soft.

2 Add the peas, potato, milk and enough water to just cover the vegetables. Simmer for about 15 minutes, or until the peas and potato are tender and the liquid has evaporated. Season with salt and freshly ground pepper.

3 Add the spring onions and fennel leaves. Roughly break up the mixture using a potato masher or fork. Serve hot, drizzled with extra virgin olive oil.

Beans in Herb Cream Sauce

Serves 4

30 g (1 oz) butter
1 garlic clove, crushed
20 green beans, trimmed
60 ml (2 fl oz/¼ cup) pouring (whipping) cream
2 teaspoons chopped rosemary
1 tablespoon snipped chives
1 teaspoon chopped thyme

1 Heat the butter in a frying pan or wok over medium heat. Add the garlic and beans and cook for 2–3 minutes, or until just tender.

2 Stir in the cream, rosemary, chives and thyme and cook for a further 1 minute. Serve hot.

Potato Salad Spring Onion Mash Roasted Ve

Roots and shoots

Salad Parsley Carrots Spiced Baby Turnips

Honey-Glazed Carrots

Serves 4

2 carrots, sliced diagonally
30 g (1 oz) butter
2 teaspoons honey
snipped chives, to serve

1 Steam the carrot over a saucepan of boiling water until tender.

2 Place the butter and honey in a small saucepan and cook over low heat until combined.

3 Pour the butter and honey mixture over the carrot and toss to combine. Sprinkle the chives over the top. Serve hot.

 Don't store carrots near apples, pears or potatoes as the ethylene gas produced by these fruits and vegetables causes carrots to turn bitter.

Asparagus with Prosciutto and Hollandaise Sauce

Serves 4

1 egg yolk
1 teaspoon lemon juice
1 teaspoon white wine vinegar
60 g (2¹/4 oz) unsalted butter, melted
20 asparagus spears, trimmed
1 slice prosciutto, cut into 4 long strips

1   Whisk together the egg yolk, lemon juice, white wine vinegar and 1 teaspoon of water. Put in the top of a double boiler over simmering water, making sure it does not touch the water. Whisk for 1 minute, or until thick and foaming.

2   Slowly pour in the melted unsalted butter, whisking constantly. Continue whisking for about 1 minute, or until thick and creamy, then season with salt and pepper.

3   Steam the asparagus spears over a saucepan of simmering water until *al dente* (about 4–8 minutes, depending on the size and age of the asparagus). Group the asparagus into 4 bundles.

4   Cook the prosciutto under a hot grill (broiler) until just starting to bubble. Wrap a strip of prosciutto around the middle of each asparagus bundle. Serve with the hollandaise sauce spooned over the bundles.

Spring Onion Mash

Serves 4–6

1 kg (2 lb 4 oz) all-purpose potatoes, cut into chunks
40 g (1¹/2 oz) butter
80 ml (2¹/2 fl oz/¹/3 cup) milk
60 ml (2 fl oz/¹/4 cup) pouring (whipping) cream
3 spring onions (scallions), thinly sliced

1 Cook the potato in a large saucepan of boiling water until tender. Drain and briefly return the potato to the heat, shaking the pan to remove any excess moisture.

2 Add the butter, milk and cream to the pan and mash the potato until smooth. Stir in the spring onion, season to taste and serve warm.

Tarragon Potatoes

Serves 6–8

500 g (1 lb 2 oz) baby new potatoes, cut in halves
2 egg yolks, lightly beaten
2 tablespoons sour cream
185 ml (6 fl oz/3/4 cup) olive oil
2 tablespoons white vinegar
1/2 teaspoon caster (superfine) sugar
1 teaspoon finely chopped tarragon or snipped chives
2 tablespoons pine nuts, roasted

1 Cook the potatoes in a large saucepan of boiling water until just tender. Drain and allow to cool.

2 Place the egg yolks in a food processor bowl. Add the sour cream and process until smooth. Gradually add the oil while the motor is running. Add the vinegar, sugar, tarragon or chives and freshly ground black pepper to taste. Process to combine.

3 Combine the tarragon mixture and potatoes in a serving dish. Serve sprinkled with the pine nuts.

New potatoes are best eaten soon after purchase, so buy in smaller quantities.

Roasted Beetroot Salad

Serves 4

2 tablespoons red wine vinegar
80 ml (2 1/2 fl oz/1/3 cup) walnut oil
1 garlic clove, crushed
1 teaspoon dijon mustard
12 French shallots
12 garlic cloves
6 beetroot (beets), scrubbed well
1 tablespoon vegetable oil
70 g (2 1/2 oz/2 cups) baby beetroot (beet) leaves
50 g (1 3/4 oz/1/2 cup) walnuts, roasted

1. Preheat the oven to 200°C (400°F/Gas 6). Combine the red wine vinegar, walnut oil, garlic and dijon mustard in a small bowl and whisk. Season well with sea salt and pepper. Set aside.

2. Put the shallots, garlic and beetroot in a large ovenproof dish and roast for 1 hour. Remove the shallots and garlic and set aside. Return the beetroot to the oven for a further 30 minutes, or until tender when pierced with a skewer.

3. Slip the shallots and garlic from their skin, and cut the beetroot into wedges. Add the dressing to the vegetables, toss together, and cool to room temperature.

4. In a large bowl, place the beet leaves, walnuts and vegetables with the dressing. Season well with sea salt and pepper and gently toss to combine. Arrange on a serving platter to serve.

Leeks à la Grecque

Serves 4

60 ml (2 fl oz/¼ cup) extra virgin olive oil

1½ tablespoons white wine

1 tablespoon tomato passata (puréed tomatoes)

¼ teaspoon sugar

1 bay leaf

1 thyme sprig

1 garlic clove, crushed

4 coriander seeds, crushed

4 peppercorns

8 small leeks, trimmed

1 teaspoon lemon juice

1 tablespoon chopped flat-leaf (Italian) parsley

1 Put the oil, wine, tomato passata, sugar, bay leaf, thyme, garlic, coriander seeds, peppercorns and 250 ml (9 fl oz/1 cup) water in a large frying pan. Bring to the boil, cover and simmer for 5 minutes.

2 Add the leeks in a single layer and bring to simmering point. Reduce the heat, cover and cook for 20–30 minutes, or until the leeks are tender (to test, pierce with a fine skewer). Lift out the leeks with a slotted spoon and put them in a serving dish.

3 Add the lemon juice to the cooking liquid and boil rapidly until the liquid is slightly syrupy. Remove the bay leaf, thyme and peppercorns. Season with salt and pour over the leeks. Serve the leeks cold, sprinkled with chopped parsley.

Spiced Potatoes

Serves 6

1.5 kg (3 lb 5 oz) roasting potatoes, peeled, cut into 4 cm (1½ in) pieces
2 tablespoons ghee
2 teaspoons ground fenugreek
1 garlic clove, crushed
1 teaspoon finely grated ginger
1 tablespoon black mustard seeds
pinch of saffron threads
80 g (2¾ oz) baby English spinach leaves

1 Preheat the oven to 180°C (350°F/Gas 4). Boil the potatoes in a large saucepan of boiling salted water until just tender, then drain.

2 Melt the ghee in a small frying pan over medium heat. Cook the fenugreek, garlic, ginger, mustard seeds and saffron. Season with salt and stir, for about 1 minute, or until fragrant.

3 Place the potatoes in a large roasting tin, add the spice mixture and toss to coat the potatoes. Bake for 1 hour, or until the potatoes are lightly browned. Remove from the oven, toss the spinach through the potatoes and serve immediately.

Purée of Swedes

Serves 4

1 kg (2 lb 4 oz) swedes (rutabaga), chopped
1 teaspoon salt
50 g (1³/4 oz) butter
1 tablespoon crème fraîche

1. Put the swede in a large saucepan, half-cover with water and add the salt and 20 g (³/4 oz) of the butter. Bring to the boil, then reduce the heat. Cover and simmer for 30 minutes, or until tender. Drain, reserving the cooking liquid.

2. Process the swede in a food processor or blender with enough of the cooking liquid to make a purée. Spoon into a saucepan and stir in the remaining butter and the crème fraîche. Reheat gently for 2–3 minutes, stirring constantly.

 Choose unblemished swedes with a purplish top and fresh green stalk for the finest flavour. Swedes can be stored in the refrigerator for up to 10 days, though their flesh will soften and their flavour strengthen.

Barbecued Baby Potatoes

Serves 6

750 g (1 lb 10 oz) baby new potatoes, unpeeled
2 tablespoons olive oil
2 tablespoons thyme
2 teaspoons crushed sea salt

1 Cut any large potatoes in half so that they are all the same size
for even cooking. Boil the potatoes in a large saucepan of boiling
salted water until just tender. Drain and lightly dry with paper towels.

2 Put the potatoes in a large bowl and add the oil and thyme. Toss
gently and leave for 1 hour.

3 Lightly oil a barbecue flat plate and preheat it to high heat. Cook
the potatoes for 15 minutes, turning frequently and brushing
with the remaining oil and thyme mixture, until golden brown.
Sprinkle with salt to serve.

 The potatoes can be left in the marinade for
up to 2 hours before barbecuing, but should
be served as soon as they are cooked.

Stir-fried Asparagus with Sesame Seeds

Serves 4

1 tablespoon sesame seeds
2 tablespoons oil
1 garlic clove, finely chopped
1 teaspoon grated fresh ginger
750 g (1 lb 10 oz) asparagus, trimmed and cut into 5 cm (2 in) pieces
1/2 teaspoon soft brown sugar
2 teaspoons sesame oil
1 tablespoon soy sauce

1   Heat a wok or frying pan over high heat. Add the sesame seeds and stir-fry for 2 minutes, or until golden. Remove from the wok and set aside.

2   Heat the oil in the wok and add the garlic, ginger and asparagus. Stir-fry over high heat for 3 minutes or until almost tender. Add the sugar and season mwith freshly ground black pepper. Stir-fry over high heat for 1 minute.

3   Sprinkle with the sesame oil, soy sauce and sesame seeds and serve immediately.

Celeriac Remoulade

Serves 4

juice of 1 lemon
2 celeriac, trimmed and peeled
2 tablespoons capers, rinsed and drained
5 cornichons, chopped
2 tablespoons finely chopped flat-leaf (Italian) parsley

MUSTARD MAYONNAISE
2 egg yolks
1 tablespoon white wine vinegar or lemon juice
1 tablespoon dijon mustard
150 ml (5 fl oz) light olive oil

1   Pour 1 litre (35 fl oz/4 cups) cold water into a large bowl and add half the lemon juice. Roughly grate the celeriac, then place in the acidulated water. Bring a saucepan of water to the boil and add the remaining lemon juice. Drain the celeriac and add to the boiling water. After 1 minute, drain and cool under running water. Pat dry with paper towels.

2   To make the mustard mayonnaise, put the egg yolks, vinegar or lemon juice and mustard in a bowl and whisk together. Add the oil, drop by drop from the tip of a teaspoon, whisking constantly until it begins to thicken, then add the oil in a very thin stream. Season and, if necessary, thin with a little warm water.

3   Toss the celeriac in a bowl with the mayonnaise, capers, cornichons and parsley.

Purée of Jerusalem Artichokes

Serves 4

750 g (1 lb 10 oz) Jerusalem artichokes, peeled
250 g (9 oz) all-purpose potatoes, cut in halves
20 g (³/₄ oz) butter
2 tablespoons crème fraîche

1 Cook the artichokes in a large saucepan of boiling salted water for 20 minutes, or until tender. Drain, then transfer to a food processor or blender and purée.

2 Cook the potatoes in a large saucepan of boiling salted water for 20 minutes, then drain and mash. Add to the artichoke with the butter and crème fraîche. Season, beat well and serve immediately.

 Jerusalem artichokes should be put in acidulated water once cut to stop them going brown, and always cooked in a non-reactive pan. Peel using a decent-sized knife and treat the Jerusalem artichoke as though it were a pineapple – just take off the top and slice down around the curve for a perfectly peeled specimen.

Parsley Carrots

Serves 6–8

600 g (1 lb 5 oz) baby carrots
2 teaspoons olive oil
30 g (1 oz) butter
2 tablespoons finely chopped flat-leaf (Italian) parsley

1 Bring a saucepan of salted water to the boil and blanch the carrots for 3 minutes, or until they start to soften. Drain, refresh under cold water and pat dry with paper towels. Toss the carrots in olive oil and season with salt and pepper.

2 Preheat a barbecue chargrill plate to medium heat and cook the carrots for 5 minutes, or until they are charred and golden all over. Toss the carrots with the butter and parsley until they are well coated. Season to taste with salt and freshly ground black pepper.

Garlic Potatoes

serves 6

60 g (2¼ oz) butter
6 large all-purpose potatoes, cubed
2 garlic cloves, crushed
60 g (2¼ oz/½ cup) grated cheddar cheese
2 tablespoons grated parmesan cheese
1 tablespoon chopped rosemary

1 Preheat the oven to 180°C (350°F/Gas 4). Melt the butter in a shallow frying pan. Add the potato and garlic and cook over medium–high heat, stirring frequently, for 5 minutes, or until golden.

2 Transfer to a shallow ovenproof dish. Sprinkle with the combined cheeses and rosemary. Bake for 45 minutes, or until the potato is tender.

Garlic is freshest in the summer when the bulbs are firm. Choose fresh, plump-looking bulbs with a white skin; store in a cool, open place.

Chargrilled Sweet Potato with Baby Leeks and Shaved Fennel

Serves 4

100 ml (3½ fl oz) olive oil
2 teaspoons chopped mint
1 garlic clove, crushed
1 small (about 400 g/14 oz) orange sweet potato
400 g (14 oz) baby leeks, trimmed and cut into 7 cm (2¾ in) lengths
1 baby fennel bulb
1 small red onion, thinly sliced
80 g (2¾ oz/scant ½ cup) kalamata olives
60 ml (2 fl oz/¼ cup) olive oil
1 tablespoon lemon juice
1 tablespoon mint

1 Combine the olive oil, mint, garlic and freshly ground black pepper in a bowl. Scrub the orange sweet potato but do not peel. Cut into 1 cm (½ in) slices, then cut the slices into half-moon shapes. Toss in the oil mixture. Add the leek to the sweet potato and toss to coat.

2 Preheat a barbecue or chargrill pan to medium–high and fry the sweet potato for 4–5 minutes. Add the leek and continue frying for 3–4 minutes, or until the vegetables are tender. Transfer to a bowl.

3 Trim the fennel bulb, reserving a few green fronds. Slice the fennel very thinly or shave it vertically into whole slices and put it in a bowl with the sweet potato and leek.

4   Add the onion, olives, olive oil, lemon juice, mint and the chopped
    fennel fronds to the vegetables. Season with salt and black pepper
    and toss to combine.

 Sweet potatoes don't keep for as long as
potatoes but will last for 1 week if stored in
a cool, dry place.

Parsnip Purée

Serves 4–6

500 g (1 lb 2 oz) parsnip, roughly chopped
50 g (1³/4 oz) butter
1 garlic clove, crushed
125 ml (4 fl oz/¹/2 cup) chicken stock
80 ml (2¹/2 fl oz/¹/3 cup) pouring (whipping) cream

1 Add the parsnip to a saucepan of boiling water and cook until tender. Drain well and transfer to a food processor.

2 Melt the butter in a frying pan, then add the garlic and cook for 2 minutes, or until the butter is a nutty brown colour. Add the butter and garlic to the food processor with the chicken stock and cream. Process until smooth and creamy. Season with sea salt and freshly ground black pepper.

 When buying parsnips, choose firm, smooth vegetables. Parsnips will keep in the refrigerator for about 4 weeks.

Hasselback Potatoes

Serves 6

8 all-purpose potatoes (1.8 kg/4 lb), cut into halves
60 g (2¼ oz) butter, melted
1 tablespoon fresh white breadcrumbs
85 g (3 oz/⅔ cup) grated cheddar cheese
½ teaspoon sweet paprika

1 Preheat the oven to 210°C (415°F/Gas 6–7). Brush a shallow ovenproof dish with a little of the melted butter.

2 Place each potato cut-side down on a board. Using a small, sharp knife, make thin cuts into the potato, taking care not to cut right through. Place the potatoes, cut side up, in the prepared dish. Brush with the melted butter. Bake for 30 minutes, brushing occasionally with butter.

3 Sprinkle with the combined breadcrumbs, cheese and paprika. Bake for a further 15 minutes, or until golden brown. Serve immediately.

Rosemary and Garlic Roasted Potatoes

Serves 4–6

1.5 kg (3 lb 5 oz) all-purpose potatoes, cut into large chunks
80 ml (2¹/₂ fl oz/¹/₃ cup) olive oil
12 garlic cloves, unpeeled
2 tablespoons rosemary

1   Preheat the oven to 200°C (400°F/Gas 6). Cook the potatoes in a
large saucepan of boiling salted water for 10 minutes, or until just
tender. Drain well.

2   Meanwhile, pour the olive oil into a large roasting tray and heat in
the oven for 5 minutes. Add the potatoes to the tray (they should
sizzle in the hot oil). Add the garlic and rosemary and season with
salt and pepper. Roast, stirring occasionally, for about 1 hour, or until
golden and crisp. Serve the potatoes with the roasted garlic cloves
popped from their skin and the rosemary.

Honey-Roasted Root Vegetables

Serves 4

60 g (2¼ oz) butter
2 tablespoons honey
4 thyme sprigs
3 carrots, cut into chunks
2 parsnips, cut into chunks
1 orange sweet potato, cut into chunks
1 white sweet potato, cut into chunks
8 baby onions, peeled
8 Jerusalem artichokes, peeled
1 garlic bulb

1 Preheat the oven to 200°C (400°F/ Gas 6). Melt the butter in a large baking dish over medium heat. Add the honey and thyme and stir. Remove from the heat and add the carrot, parsnip, orange and white sweet potato, onions and Jerusalem artichokes. Season well with salt and freshly ground black pepper and gently toss to coat with the honey butter.

2 Trim the base of the garlic and wrap the bulb in foil. Add to the baking dish and place in the oven for 1 hour, turning the vegetables occasionally. When cooked, remove the foil from the garlic and squeeze the cloves from their skin. Add to the other vegetables and serve.

Jerusalem Artichokes Roasted with Red Wine and Garlic

Serves 4

800 g (1 lb 12 oz) Jerusalem artichokes
1 tablespoon lemon juice
2 tablespoons red wine
2 tablespoons olive oil
1 tablespoon tamari
2 garlic cloves, crushed
2–3 drops Tabasco sauce
2 tablespoons vegetable stock
2 tablespoons chopped flat-leaf (Italian) parsley

1   Preheat the oven to 200°C (400°F/Gas 6). Scrub the artichokes well, then cut in half lengthways, and put in a bowl of water mixed with the lemon juice. Drain and dry the artichoke halves with paper towels.

2   Combine the red wine, olive oil, tamari, garlic, Tabasco sauce and stock in a baking dish. Place the artichokes in the dish and toss to combine. Season with salt and freshly ground black pepper.

3   Bake, covered, for 40 minutes, or until tender, then uncover and bake for a further 5 minutes or until the juices have formed a reduced glaze. Remove from the oven and toss with the parsley before serving.

Dauphine Potatoes

Serves 4-6

600 g (1 lb 5 oz) all-purpose potatoes, quartered
50 g (1³/4 oz) butter
60 g (2¹/4 oz/¹/2 cup) plain (all-purpose) flour
3 eggs, lightly beaten
oil, for deep-frying

1 Cook the potatoes in a large saucepan of boiling salted water until just tender. Drain well and mash until smooth.

2 Place the butter and 125 ml (4 fl oz/¹/2 cup) water in a large saucepan and bring to the boil. Add the flour and stir with a wooden spoon until the mixture comes away from the side and forms a ball. Transfer to a bowl and allow to cool for 30 minutes.

3 Add the egg, a little at a time, and beat well after each addition using electric beaters. Mix in the potatoes and season. Fill a deep heavy-based frying pan one-third full of oil and heat to 180°C (350°F), or until a cube of bread dropped in the oil browns in 15 seconds. Using two dessert spoons, mould the mixture into quenelles (ovals) and drop into the oil one at a time. Fry for 1 minute, or until golden brown. Drain on paper towels.

Duchess Potatoes

Serves 4

500 g (1 lb 2 oz) all-purpose potatoes, peeled
55 g (2 oz) butter
2 egg yolks
2–3 tablespoons milk

1 Cook the potatoes in a large saucepan of boiling salted water until just tender. Drain well.

2 Preheat the oven to 180°C (350°F/Gas 4). Add the butter and egg yolks to the potatoes and mash until smooth. Add enough milk to make a soft potato purée that will hold its shape. Season to taste.

3 Spoon the potato into a piping bag and pipe rosettes of potato onto a lightly buttered baking tray. Bake in the oven until browned on top.

 Duchess potatoes can also be used as a garnish for roasts, a decorative border for savoury dishes or as a topping for cottage pies.

Deep-fried Parmesan Carrots

Serves 6

500 g (1 lb 2 oz) baby carrots
60 g (2¼ oz/½ cup) plain (all-purpose) flour
2 teaspoons ground cumin
2 eggs
250 g (9 oz/3 cups) fine fresh white breadcrumbs
1 tablespoon chopped flat-leaf (Italian) parsley
65 g (2¼ oz/⅔ cup) finely grated parmesan cheese
oil, for deep-frying

1   Trim the leafy carrot tops, leaving about 2 cm (¾ in). Bring a large saucepan of water to the boil, add 1 teaspoon of salt and cook the carrots for 5 minutes, or until tender. Drain, dry well with paper towels and allow to cool.

2   Sift the flour and cumin onto a sheet of baking paper, then beat the eggs together in a wide, shallow bowl. Combine the breadcrumbs, parsley and parmesan, and season with salt and pepper. Roll the carrots in the flour, then the eggs and finally the breadcrumbs.

3   Fill a deep, heavy-based saucepan one-third full of oil and heat until a cube of bread dropped into the oil browns in 20 seconds. Deep-fry the carrots in batches until golden and crisp. Serve immediately.

Honeyed Baby Turnips with Lemon Thyme

Serves 4

500 g (1 lb 2 oz) baby turnips
40 g (1¹/₂ oz) butter
60 g (2¹/₄ oz/¹/₄ cup) honey
3 teaspoons lemon juice
¹/₂ teaspoon grated lemon zest
3 teaspoons chopped lemon thyme

1 Lightly scrub the turnips under water. Trim the tips and stalks. Cook in a saucepan of boiling water for 1 minute. Drain, refresh under cold water, then drain again.

2 Heat the butter in a saucepan and add the honey. Bring the mixture to the boil. Add the lemon juice and zest. Boil over high heat for 3 minutes. Add the turnips to the honey and lemon mixture. Cook over high heat for 3 minutes, or until the turnips are almost tender and well glazed.

3 Add the lemon thyme, then remove the pan from the heat. Toss until the turnips are well coated. Serve warm.

 Store turnips unwashed and refrigerated in a perforated plastic bag for up to 2 weeks.

Asparagus Gremolata

serves 4

50 g (1³/4 oz) butter
80 g (2³/4 oz/1 cup) coarse fresh white breadcrumbs
1 small handful chopped flat-leaf (Italian) parsley
2 garlic cloves, very finely chopped
3 teaspoons finely chopped lemon zest
400 g (14 oz) green asparagus, trimmed
1¹/2 tablespoons virgin olive oil

1 Melt the butter in a heavy-based frying pan over high heat. Add
   the breadcrumbs and, using a wooden spoon, stir until the crumbs
   are golden and crisp. Remove to a plate to cool slightly.

2 Combine the parsley, garlic and lemon zest in a bowl, add the
   breadcrumbs, and season to taste with freshly ground black pepper.

3 Bring a large, wide saucepan of water to the boil, add the asparagus
   and cook for 2–3 minutes, or until just tender when pierced with
   a fine skewer. Drain well and arrange on a warmed serving plate.
   Drizzle with the olive oil and sprinkle gremolata over the top.

Moroccan Spiced Carrot Salad

Serves 4–6

2 cardamom pods

1 teaspoon black mustard seeds

1/2 teaspoon ground cumin

1/2 teaspoon ground ginger

1 teaspoon paprika

1/2 teaspoon ground coriander

4 large carrots, grated

80 ml (2 1/2 fl oz/1/3 cup) olive oil

1 tablespoon lemon juice

2 tablespoons orange juice

35 g (1 1/4 oz/1/4 cup) currants

25 g (1 oz/1/2 cup) finely chopped coriander (cilantro) leaves

2 tablespoons finely chopped pistachio nuts

1 teaspoon orange flower water

250 g (9 oz/1 cup) Greek-style yoghurt

1 Crush the cardamom pods to extract the seeds. Discard the pods. Heat a frying pan over low heat and cook the mustard seeds for a few seconds, or until they start to pop. Add the cumin, ginger, paprika, cardamom and ground coriander, and heat for 5 seconds, or until fragrant. Remove from the heat and stir in the oil, citrus juices and currants until combined.

2 Put the carrot in a large bowl. Pour the spiced oil over the carrot and leave for 30 minutes. Add the coriander and toss to combine. Pile the salad onto a serving dish and garnish with the pistachios. Combine the orange flower water and yoghurt and serve separately.

Herbed Potato Salad

Serves 4

650 g (1 lb 5 oz) red-skinned potatoes, unpeeled, scrubbed and
   cut into cubes
1 red onion, thinly sliced
1 tablespoon chopped mint
1 tablespoon chopped flat-leaf (Italian) parsley
1 tablespoon snipped chives
90 g (3¼ oz/⅓ cup) whole-egg mayonnaise
90 g (3¼ oz/⅓ cup) plain yoghurt

1 Cook the potato in a large saucepan of boiling water until just tender.
   Drain and allow to cool completely.

2 Put the potatoes, onion and herbs in a large bowl. Combine the
   mayonnaise and yoghurt, then gently mix through to combine.

Store potatoes in paper bags to allow
moisture to escape and to keep light out.
Keep in a cool and dry, dark, well-ventilated
place to prevent them from sprouting.

Potato and Leek Gratin

Serves 4

60 g (2¼ oz) butter
400 g (14 oz) leeks, trimmed, cut in half and sliced
3 garlic cloves, thinly sliced
1 tablespoon chopped thyme
1 kg (2 lb 4 oz) all-purpose potatoes, thinly sliced
350 g (12 oz) mascarpone cheese
250 ml (9 fl oz/1 cup) vegetable stock

1 Preheat the oven to 180°C (350°F/Gas 4). Melt the butter in a saucepan and cook the leek for 10 minutes, or until soft. Season, add the garlic and thyme and cook for 2–3 minutes. Grease a 20 cm (8 in) round gratin dish with butter.

2 Arrange a layer of potato in the base of the dish and season with salt and pepper. Scatter with 3 tablespoons of leek and a few dollops of mascarpone. Continue the layers, finishing with a layer of potato and some mascarpone. Pour the stock over the top and cover with foil.

3 Bake for 45 minutes, then remove the foil and bake for a further 15 minutes to brown the top.

Beetroot Mash

Serves 4

1 kg (2 lb 4 oz) all-purpose potatoes
1 kg (2 lb 4 oz) beetroot (beets)
snipped chives, to garnish
20 g (³/4 oz) butter

1 Cook the potatoes in a large saucepan of boiling salted water until just tender. Drain well.

2 To prepare the beetroot, cut off the leaves, leaving 3 cm (1¹/4 in) of stalk above the bulb. Wash carefully, but don't peel. Boil until tender (this can take up to 2 hours), rub off the skins and mash with the potatoes. Season well. Add the chives and butter to serve.

When cooking beetroot, take care to prevent it from bleeding. Don't cut or peel before they are cooked as the skin and root must be intact when cooked or the beetroot will 'bleed' and lose its colour. Wash them carefully to prevent the skin breaking. Store beetroot in the refrigerator for up to 2 weeks.

Spiced Baby Turnips

Serves 4

400 g (14 oz) small roma (plum) tomatoes
60 ml (2 fl oz/¼ cup) olive oil
3 small onions, sliced
3 teaspoons ground coriander
1 teaspoon sweet paprika
350 g (12 oz) baby turnips, trimmed
1 teaspoon soft brown sugar
1 handful flat-leaf (Italian) parsley
600 g (1 lb 5 oz) silverbeet (Swiss chard)

1 Cut the core from each tomato and score a cross in the base. Place in a heatproof bowl and cover with boiling water. Leave for 30 seconds, then transfer to cold water and peel the skin away from the cross. Cut the tomatoes into 1.5 cm (⁵⁄₈ in) slices and gently squeeze out most of the juice and seeds.

2 Heat the olive oil in a large frying pan over medium heat and fry the onion for 5–6 minutes, or until soft. Stir in the coriander and paprika. Cook for 1 minute, then add the tomato, turnips, sugar and 4 tablespoons hot water. Season well with salt and pepper. Cook over medium heat for 5 minutes.

3 Cover the pan, reduce the heat to low and cook for 4–5 minutes, or until the turnips are tender.

4 Meanwhile, strip the silverbeet leaves off the stalks, discarding the stalks, to give about 250 g (9 oz) of leaves. Rinse under cold water and shake off the excess water.

5 Stir the parsley and silverbeet into the pan, check the seasoning and cook, covered, for 4 minutes, or until the silverbeet is wilted. Serve hot.

 Store turnips unwashed and refrigerated in a perforated plastic bag for up to 2 weeks.

Creamy Sweet Potato Polenta

Serves 4

400 g (14 oz) white sweet potato, cut into chunks
40 g (1¹/₂ oz) butter
60 ml (2 fl oz/¹/₄ cup) pouring (whipping) cream
1 teaspoon salt
110 g (3³/₄ oz/³/₄ cup) instant polenta
cayenne pepper, to sprinkle

1 Cook the sweet potato in a saucepan of boiling salted water for 15 minutes, or until tender. Drain, then mash with the butter and cream.

2 Bring 750 ml (26 fl oz/3 cups) water to the boil in a heavy-based saucepan. Add the salt and slowly stir in the polenta, breaking up any lumps as you stir. Cook over medium–low heat, stirring often, for 8–10 minutes.

3 Stir the sweet potato mash into the polenta and continue cooking and stirring until the polenta is very thick and pulls away from the side of the pan. Remove from the heat and season with salt and white pepper. Serve with a sprinkling of cayenne pepper on top.

Sautéed Potatoes

Serves 4–6

1 kg (2 lb 4 oz) all-purpose potatoes, cut into 2 cm (3/4 in) cubes
80 ml (2 1/2 fl oz/1/3 cup) olive oil
2 bacon slices, chopped
1 onion, chopped
2 spring onions (scallions), sliced
1 tablespoon thyme
1 garlic clove, crushed

1 Cook the potatoes in a large saucepan of boiling salted water for 5 minutes. Drain well, then dry on a clean tea towel (dish towel).

2 Heat the oil in a large heavy-based frying pan. Add the bacon, onion and spring onion and cook for 5 minutes. Add the potato and gently cook over low heat, shaking the pan occasionally, for about 20 minutes, or until tender. Turn the potato frequently to prevent sticking and partially cover the pan halfway through cooking so that the steam will help cook the potato through.

3 Add the thyme, garlic and some salt and freshly ground black pepper in the last few minutes of cooking. Increase the heat at the end to crisp the potatoes if necessary.

Potato Cake

Serves 4–6

30 g (1 oz) butter
2 tablespoons olive oil
1 garlic clove, crushed
1/2 teaspoon freshly ground black pepper
200 g (7 oz/2 cups) dried breadcrumbs
125 g (41/2 oz/1 cup) grated cheddar cheese, plus extra for topping
50 g (13/4 oz/1/2 cup) freshly grated parmesan cheese
8 all-purpose potatoes, thinly sliced

1   Preheat the oven to 180°C (350°F/Gas 4). Lightly grease a deep
    20 cm (8 in) spring-form tin and line the base and side with
    baking paper.

2   Heat the butter and oil in a small saucepan. Add the garlic
    and pepper.

3   Combine the breadcrumbs and cheddar and parmesan cheeses
    in a bowl.

4   Overlap some potato slices in the base of tin. Brush with the butter
    mixture. Sprinkle with some of the breadcrumb mixture. Continue
    layering. Top with the extra cheddar cheese. Press down firmly. Bake
    for 1 hour, or until top is lightly browned.

Mashed Carrots with Cumin Seeds

Serves 4

6 carrots, cut into chunks
1 tablespoon olive oil
2 garlic cloves, finely chopped
1 teaspoon ground turmeric
2 teaspoons finely grated fresh ginger
60 g (2¼ oz/¼ cup) Greek-style yoghurt
2 teaspoons ready-made harissa
2 tablespoons chopped coriander (cilantro) leaves
2 teaspoons lime juice
1 teaspoon cumin seeds

1   Put the carrot in a large saucepan and cover with cold water. Bring to the boil, then reduce the heat and simmer for 3 minutes. Drain and allow to dry.

2   Heat the olive oil in a heavy-based, non-stick saucepan. Cook the garlic, turmeric and ginger over medium heat for 1 minute, or until fragrant. Add the carrots, and cook for 3 minutes. Stir in 1 tablespoon water and cook, covered, over low heat for 10–15 minutes, or until the carrots are soft. Transfer the mixture to a bowl and roughly mash.

3   Add the yoghurt, harissa, coriander and lime juice to the carrot mixture and stir to combine. Season to taste with salt and freshly ground black pepper.

4   Heat a heavy-based frying pan over medium heat. Add the cumin seeds and dry-fry for 1–2 minutes, or until fragrant. Scatter over the mashed carrots.

Balsamic Mixed Onions

Serves 4

250 ml (9 fl oz/1 cup) dry white wine
125 ml (4 fl oz/1/2 cup) balsamic vinegar
1 tablespoon olive oil
2 tablespoons light brown sugar
2 dried bay leaves
1 kg (2 lb 4 oz) assorted small onions
30 g (1 oz/1/4 cup) raisins

1 Put the wine, balsamic vinegar, olive oil, sugar and bay leaf in a large saucepan with 2 tablespoons water and bring to the boil. Peel the onions but leave the ends intact; just cut off any roots. Add to the pan and return to the boil.

2 Add the raisins and simmer gently, tossing occasionally, for 50 minutes, or until the onions are tender and the liquid is thick and syrupy. Transfer to a serving dish and serve at room temperature.

 Store in a covered container in the refrigerator for up to 2 weeks.

Piquant Potato Salad

Serves 4

500 g (1 lb 2 oz) baby new potatoes
2 teaspoons chopped dill
2 spring onions (scallions), chopped
1 tablespoon capers, rinsed, drained and coarsely chopped
2 tablespoons extra virgin olive oil
1¹/2 tablespoons lemon juice
1 teaspoon finely grated orange zest

1 Put the potatoes in a large saucepan of salted water and bring to the boil. Cook for 10 minutes, or until tender. Drain well.

2 Put the potatoes in a bowl with the dill, spring onion, capers and salt and pepper. Mix well to combine. Whisk together the oil, lemon juice and orange zest in a small jug and pour over the hot potatoes. Toss to coat the potatoes and serve warm.

 Any small potato works well in this delicious salad. You can choose from those which are readily available such as bintje (yellow finn) or kipfler (fingerling).

Vichy Carrots

Serves 4

800 g (1 lb 12 oz) baby carrots, thinly sliced
$^1/_2$ teaspoon salt
$^1/_2$ teaspoon sugar
finely chopped flat-leaf (Italian) parsley, to serve
20 g ($^3/_4$ oz) butter, plus extra to serve

1 Put the carrot in a shallow frying pan and cover with water. Add the salt, sugar and butter.

2 Cover and cook over low heat until the carrots are nearly tender. Remove the lid and boil until any remaining liquid evaporates. Serve sprinkled with the parsley and extra butter.

Spiced Sweet Potato Purée

Serves 4-6

500 g (1 lb 2 oz) sweet potatoes, chopped
50 g (1³/4 oz) butter
1 teaspoon ground cumin
1 teaspoon garam masala
1 onion, finely chopped
80 ml (2¹/2 fl oz/¹/3 cup) orange juice
125 ml (4 fl oz/¹/2 cup) pouring (whipping) cream

1 Cook the sweet potato in a large saucepan of boiling water until tender. Drain and transfer to a food processor.

2 Melt the butter in a frying pan. Add the cumin, garam masala and onion. Cook over medium heat for 5 minutes, or until the onion is soft and golden. Add the onion mixture to the food processor with the orange juice and cream. Process until smooth and creamy.

Chargrilled Asparagus with Salsa

Serves 4-6

3 eggs
2 tablespoons milk
1 tablespoon olive oil
2 corn cobs
1 small red onion, diced
1 red capsicum (pepper), finely chopped
2 tablespoons chopped thyme
2 tablespoons olive oil, extra
2 tablespoons balsamic vinegar
24 fresh asparagus spears
1 tablespoon macadamia oil

1　Beat the eggs and milk to combine. Heat the oil in a non-stick frying pan over medium heat, add the egg and cook until just set. Flip and cook the other side. Remove and allow to cool, then roll up and cut into thin slices.

2　Cook the corn in a chargrill pan (griddle) until tender. Allow to cool slightly, then slice off the corn kernels. Make the salsa by gently combining the corn, onion, capsicum, thyme, extra olive oil and balsamic vinegar.

3　Trim off any woody ends from the asparagus spears, lightly brush with macadamia oil and cook in a chargrill pan (griddle) or on a barbecue hotplate until tender.

4　Serve the asparagus topped with a little salsa and the egg.

Roasted Beetroot and Whole Garlic

Serves 4

3 small beetroot (beets)
1 tablespoon balsamic vinegar
100 ml (3^1/$_2$ fl oz) olive oil
12 garlic cloves, unpeeled

1　Preheat the oven to 180°C (350°F/Gas 4). Line a roasting tin with baking paper. Wearing rubber gloves, trim the tops off the beetroot, leaving 5 cm (2 in) of the stalks intact. Thinly peel the beetroot and cut them in half lengthways. Arrange, cut side up, in the prepared tin.

2　Combine the balsamic vinegar and olive oil and drizzle half over the beetroot. Season lightly with salt and freshly ground black pepper.

3　Wrap the garlic cloves in a small sheet of foil and add to the tin. Roast for 50 minutes, then cover loosely with foil and bake for a further 45 minutes, or until the beetroot is tender.

4　Unwrap the garlic and gently squeeze the flesh out from 1 clove. Add to the remaining balsamic dressing and mix in with a fork. Transfer the beetroot to a serving dish and drizzle with the garlic dressing. Scatter over the remaining garlic cloves.

Hot Potato Salad

serves 6–8

4 bacon slices
1.5 kg (3 lb 5 oz) all-purpose potatoes, unpeeled
4 spring onions (scallions), sliced
1 small handful flat-leaf (Italian) parsley

DRESSING
170 ml (5$\frac{1}{2}$ fl oz/$\frac{2}{3}$ cup) extra virgin olive oil
1 tablespoon dijon mustard
80 ml (2$\frac{1}{2}$ fl oz/$\frac{1}{3}$ cup) white wine vinegar

1 Preheat the grill (broiler). Trim the rind and any excess fat from the bacon. Cook under the grill until crisp, then chop into small pieces.

2 Put the potatoes in a large saucepan of salted water and bring to the boil. Cook for 10–15 minutes, or until tender. Drain and cool slightly.

3 To make the dressing, whisk all the ingredients in a bowl until well combined.

4 Cut the potatoes into quarters and place in a bowl with half the bacon, the spring onion, parsely and some salt and freshly ground black pepper. Pour in half the dressing and toss to coat the potatoes.

5 Transfer the potatoes to a serving bowl, drizzle with the remaining dressing and sprinkle with the remaining bacon.

Cold Potato Salad

Serves 4

600 g (1 lb 5 oz) all-purpose potatoes, unpeeled and cut
   into bite-sized pieces
1 small onion, finely chopped
1 small green capsicum (pepper), chopped
2–3 celery stalks, chopped
1 small handful finely chopped flat-leaf (Italian) parsley

DRESSING
185 g (6^1/2 oz/^{3}/4 cup) whole-egg mayonnaise
1–2 tablespoons white wine vinegar or lemon juice
2 tablespoons sour cream

1   Put the potatoes in a large saucepan of salted water and bring to the
    boil. Cook for 5–10 minutes, or until tender. Drain and allow to cool.

2   Combine the onion, capsicum, celery and parsley with the potato in a
    large bowl, reserving some of the parsley to garnish.

3   To make the dressing, mix together all the ingredients and season
    with salt and black pepper. Pour over the salad and gently toss to
    combine. Garnish with the reserved parsley.

Waxy potatoes have a high moisture
content and are low in starch. They hold
their shape when boiled or roasted but don't
mash well. Waxy potates include roseval,
charlotte, kipfler (fingerling) and cara.

Baked Swedes with Ricotta, Blue Cheese and Sage

Serves 4

4 swedes (rutabaga), scrubbed
1 1/2 tablespoons olive oil
40 g (1 1/2 oz) butter
55 g (2 oz) creamy blue vein cheese, crumbled
125 g (4 1/2 oz/1/2 cup) ricotta cheese
12 sage leaves
1 garlic clove, crushed

1   Preheat the oven to 180°C (350°F/Gas 4). Rub the swedes with one-third of the oil. Place each in the centre of a 30 cm (12 in) square of foil, season lightly with salt and pepper and dot with the butter. Fold up the foil to enclose the swedes. Arrange, root down, in a small baking dish and bake for 1 hour, or until tender.

2   Mix the blue cheese and ricotta together in a small saucepan and heat over a low heat until soft and flowing. Keep warm. Heat the remaining olive oil in a small frying pan until hot. Fry the sage leaves until crisp. Drain on paper towels.

3   Add the garlic to the frying pan, reduce the heat to low and fry until just beginning to colour. Transfer to the cheese mixture and add 4 of the sage leaves. Season to taste with salt and freshly ground black pepper and stir to combine.

4   Remove the foil from the swedes and cut them diagonally into 2–3 cm (3/4–1 1/4 in) slices. Reassemble to serve, with the sauce spooned over the top. Top with the remaining sage leaves.

Carrot and Almond Salad

Serves 4

4 large carrots
2 tablespoons peanut oil
1 teaspoon caster (superfine) sugar
1/2 teaspoon brown mustard seeds
1/4 teaspoon curry powder
2 tablespoons lemon juice
25 g (1 oz/1/4 cup) flaked almonds, roasted
1 large handful coriander (cilantro) leaves
60 g (21/4 oz/1/4 cup) Greek-style yoghurt

1 Heat the grill (broiler) to medium. Slice the carrots thinly, on the diagonal. Put 1 tablespoon of the oil in a bowl, mix in the sugar, then add the carrot and toss to coat. Spread the carrot on a baking tray and grill (broil) for 10–15 minutes, turning occasionally, until lightly browned and tender. Remove from the heat and allow to cool, then place in a bowl.

2 Heat the remaining oil in a small frying pan. Add the mustard seeds and curry powder and cook over low heat for 1 minute, or until fragrant. Allow to cool a little, then whisk in the lemon juice and season to taste with salt and pepper.

3 Drizzle the spice mixture over the carrots, add the almonds and coriander and toss gently until well combined. Serve at room temperature, with a dollop of yoghurt.

Crisp Potatoes in Spicy Tomato Sauce

Serves 6

1 kg (2 lb 4 oz) desiree or other all-purpose potatoes
vegetable oil, for deep-frying
500 g (1 lb 2 oz) ripe roma (plum) tomatoes
2 tablespoons olive oil
1/4 red onion, finely chopped
2 garlic cloves, crushed
3 teaspoons paprika
1/4 teaspoon cayenne pepper
1 bay leaf
1 teaspoon sugar
flat-leaf (Italian) parsley, to garnish

1 Cut the potatoes into 2 cm (3/4 in) cubes. Rinse, then drain well and pat completely dry. Fill a deep-fryer or large heavy-based saucepan one-third full of oil and heat to 180°C (350°F), or until a cube of bread dropped into the oil browns in 15 seconds. Cook the potato in batches for 10 minutes, or until golden. Drain well on paper towels. Do not discard the oil.

2 Score a cross in the base of each tomato. Place in a bowl of boiling water for 10 seconds, then plunge into cold water and peel the skin away from the cross. Chop the flesh.

3 Heat the olive oil in a saucepan over medium heat and cook the onion for 3 minutes, or until softened. Add the garlic, paprika and cayenne and cook for 1–2 minutes, or until fragrant.

4   Add the tomato, bay leaf, sugar and 90 ml (3 fl oz) water, and cook, stirring occasionally, for 20 minutes, or until thick and pulpy. Cool slightly and remove the bay leaf. Blend in a food processor until smooth, adding a little water if necessary. Before serving, return the sauce to the saucepan and simmer over low heat for 2 minutes, or until heated though. Season well.

5   Reheat the oil to 180°C (350°F) and cook the potato again, in batches, for 2 minutes, or until very crisp and golden. Drain on paper towels. (This second frying makes the potato extra crispy and stops the sauce soaking in immediately.) Place on a platter and cover with the sauce. Garnish with parsley and serve.

Creamy Potato Gratin

Serves 4-6

30 g (1 oz) butter
1 onion, sliced into thin rings
750 g (1 lb 10 oz) all-purpose potatoes, thinly sliced
125 g (4¹/₂ oz/1 cup) grated cheddar cheese
375 ml (13 fl oz/1¹/₂ cups) pouring (whipping) cream

1 Preheat the oven to 180°C (350°F/Gas 4). Melt the butter in a frying pan and cook the onion for 5 minutes, or until it is soft and translucent.

2 Arrange a single layer of slightly overlapping potato slices in a lightly greased 1 litre (35 fl oz/4 cups) baking dish. Top the potato with a layer of onion rings. Divide the cheese in half and set aside one half to use for a topping. Sprinkle a little of the remaining cheese over the onion. Continue layering in this order until all the potato, onion and cheese have been used up. Sprinkle the reserved grated cheese over the top.

3 Pour the cream into a small bowl, season with some salt and freshly ground black pepper and whisk gently until combined. Pour the mixture over the layered potato and onion, then bake for 40 minutes, or until the potato is tender, the cheese has melted and the top is golden brown.

Baked Sweet Potato with Saffron and Pine Nut Butter

Serves 4–6

1 kg (2 lb 4 oz) white sweet potatoes
2 tablespoons vegetable oil
1 tablespoon milk
pinch of saffron threads
100 g (3½ oz) unsalted butter, softened
40 g (1½ oz/¼ cup) pine nuts, roasted
2 tablespoons finely chopped flat-leaf (Italian) parsley
2 garlic cloves, crushed

1 Preheat the oven to 180°C (350°F/Gas 4). Peel the sweet potatoes and cut into large chunks. Toss to coat with the oil. Put on a baking tray, cover with foil and roast for 20 minutes.

2 Warm the milk in a small saucepan, then add the saffron and leave to infuse for 5 minutes. Put the butter, milk mixture, pine nuts, parsley and garlic in a food processor and pulse to combine. Place a sheet of plastic wrap on the workbench, put the butter in the centre and roll up to form a neat log, about 4 cm (1½ in) in diameter. Refrigerate the butter for 30 minutes.

3 Remove the foil from the potatoes and roast, uncovered, for a further 30 minutes, or until they are cooked through. Bring the butter to room temperature, unwrap, cut into 1 cm (½ in) slices and return to the refrigerator to keep cool.

4 Arrange the butter slices over the sweet potato, season with salt and ground black pepper and serve.

Spicy Fried Potatoes

Serves 4

600 g (1 lb 5 oz) all-purpose potatoes, cut into 3 cm (1^1/$_4$ in) cubes
60 ml (2 fl oz/^{1}/$_4$ cup) vegetable oil
1 tablespoon panch phora
2 teaspoons ground cumin
^{1}/$_2$ teaspoon ground turmeric
^{1}/$_2$ teaspoon chilli powder
1 onion, thinly sliced
2 garlic cloves, finely chopped
1 tablespoon lime juice
2 tablespoons chopped coriander (cilantro) leaves

1   Put the potato cubes in a large saucepan of salted water and bring to the boil. Cook for 5 minutes, or until tender. Drain, refresh under cold running water and drain again. Pat dry with paper towels.

2   Heat the oil in a large non-stick frying pan. Add the panch phora and remaining spices and cook for 1 minute, or until aromatic. Stir in the onion and cook for 5 minutes over medium heat, or until the onion is cooked.

3   Add the garlic and potato cubes and stir to coat in the spices. Season with salt. Stir often and fry the potato for 15 minutes, or until the potato is cooked and golden brown. To serve, sprinkle with lime juice and the coriander leaves.

Beetroot and Chive Salad

Serves 4

24 baby beetroot (beets), unpeeled, trimmed
50 g (1³/4 oz/¹/2 cup) walnut halves
50 g (1³/4 oz/2 cups) roughly chopped picked over watercress
1¹/2 tablespoons snipped chives (2 cm/³/4 in lengths)

DRESSING
¹/4 teaspoon honey
¹/4 teaspoon dijon mustard
1 tablespoon balsamic vinegar
2 tablespoons olive oil

1 Preheat the oven to 200°C (400°F/Gas 6). Place the beetroot in a
   roasting tin, cover with foil and roast for 1 hour, or until tender.
   Remove from the oven and peel when cool enough to handle.

2 To make the dressing, combine the honey, mustard and balsamic
   vinegar in a small jug. Whisk in the oil with a fork until well
   combined, then season.

3 Reduce the oven to 180°C (350°F/Gas 4). Spread the walnuts on a
   baking tray and bake for 10 minutes, or until lightly golden. Allow
   to cool, then roughly chop the walnuts. Combine the watercress,
   beetroot and chives in a large bowl with the dressing and walnuts.

Stir-Fried Carrots with Ginger and Mint

Serves 4

600 g (1 lb 5 oz) carrots
30 g (1 oz) butter
1 teaspoon grated palm sugar (jaggery)
1 scant teaspoon grated ginger
60 ml (2 fl oz/¼ cup) mango juice
1 small handful torn mint

1 Peel the carrots and cut on the diagonal into 5 mm (¼ in) thick slices. Melt the butter in a frying pan over medium heat. Add the palm sugar, ginger and carrots. Fry, stirring constantly, for 1 minute, without browning.

2 Add the mango juice and 60 ml (2 fl oz/¼ cup) hot water, increase the heat and boil for 3–4 minutes, or until most of the liquid has evaporated. Add 1 small handful torn mint and season lightly with salt and white pepper.

Diamond-Cut Sweet Potato and Slivered Garlic

Serves 4

2 small orange sweet potatoes
juice of 1/2 orange
1 tablespoon olive oil
8–10 rosemary sprigs
2 garlic cloves, thinly sliced

1 Preheat the oven to 190°C (375°F/Gas 5). Peel the sweet potatoes and cut in half lengthways. Using a strong, sharp knife, make 1 cm (1/2 in) deep cuts in a diamond pattern in the peeled surface, 1.5–2 cm (5/8–3/4 in) apart. Be careful not to cut all the way through. Place, cut side up, on a baking tray.

2 Combine the orange juice with the olive oil in a small bowl and season well with salt and freshly ground black pepper. Drizzle all over the sweet potato. Scatter the rosemary sprigs on top and roast in the oven for 20 minutes.

3 Scatter the garlic cloves over the sweet potato and roast for a further 20–30 minutes, or until tender.

Fresh Beetroot and Goat's Cheese Salad

Serves 4

4 bulbs beetroot (beets) with leaves (about 1 kg/2 lb 4 oz)
200 g (7 oz) green beans, trimmed
1 tablespoon red wine vinegar
2 tablespoons extra virgin olive oil
1 garlic clove, crushed
1 tablespoon capers in brine, rinsed, drained and coarsely chopped
1/2 teaspoon salt
1/2 teaspoon freshly ground black pepper
100 g (3 1/2 oz) goat's cheese

1 Trim the leaves from the beetroot. Scrub the bulbs and wash the leaves well. Bring a large saucepan of water to the boil, add the beetroot, then reduce the heat and simmer, covered, for 30 minutes, or until tender. Drain and allow to cool. Peel the skins off the beetroot and cut the bulbs into wedges.

2 Meanwhile, bring a saucepan of water to the boil, add the beans and cook for 3 minutes or until just tender. Remove with tongs and plunge into a bowl of cold water. Drain well. Add the beetroot leaves to the boiling water and cook for 3–5 minutes, or until the leaves and stems are tender. Drain, plunge into a bowl of cold water, then drain.

3 To make the dressing, put the vinegar, oil, garlic, capers, salt and pepper in a jar and shake well. Divide the beans and beetroot wedges and leaves among four plates. Crumble the goat's cheese over the top and drizzle with the dressing.

Baby Baked Potatoes

Serves 6

750 g (1 lb 10 oz) baby potatoes
2 tablespoons olive oil
2 tablespoons thyme
2 teaspoons crushed sea salt

1   Wash the potatoes thoroughly under cold water. Cut any large ones in half so that they are all a uniform size for even cooking. Put the potatoes in a large saucepan of salted water and bring to the boil. Cook until tender. Drain and lightly pat them dry with paper towels.

2   Put the potatoes in a large bowl, and add the oil and thyme. Toss gently to coat the potatoes and set aside for 1 hour. Preheat the oven to 180°C (350°F/Gas 4).

3   Put the potatoes in a lightly oiled baking dish. Bake for 20 minutes, turning frequently and brushing with the remaining oil and thyme mixture, until golden brown. Put in a serving bowl and sprinkle with the salt. Garnish with extra thyme sprigs, if desired.

Glazed Turnips

Serves 4

4 turnips or 16 baby turnips
40 g (1¹/₂ oz) butter
1 tablespoon soft brown sugar

1 Peel the turnips and cut into quarters, or trim the baby turnips. Boil for 8–10 minutes, or until tender but still firm, then drain well.

2 Melt the butter in a frying pan. Add the turnips, sprinkle on the sugar and fry until the turnips are golden and caramelized (be careful the sugar does not burn).

Pink Fir Potatoes with Sesame Miso Dressing

Serves 4

750 g (1 lb 10 oz) all-purpose potatoes
1/2 teaspoon salt
1 1/2 tablespoons white miso paste
1 1/2 tablespoons lime juice
1 1/2 tablespoons honey
1 1/2 tablespoons tahini
1 teaspoon sesame oil
1 garlic clove, crushed
4 spring onions (scallions)
2 tablespoons pepitas (pumpkin seeds), peeled, roasted
1 small handful mizuna leaves
sansho pepper, to season (optional)

1 Scrub the potatoes. Put the potatoes in a large saucepan of salted water and bring to the boil. Reduce the heat and simmer for 12–15 minutes, or until just tender. Drain the potatoes and allow to cool slightly before cutting them into 2–3 cm (3/4–1 1/4 in) slices on the diagonal.

2 Meanwhile, combine the white miso paste, lime juice, honey, tahini, sesame oil, garlic and 2 tablespoons water in a large bowl. Add the potatoes.

3 Cut the spring onions into short lengths on the diagonal. Add to the bowl, along with the pepitas and mizuna leaves. Season lightly with sansho pepper, toss to coat and serve immediately.

Baby Beetroot and Tatsoi Salad with Honey Mustard Dressing

Serves 4

1.6 kg (3 lb 8 oz) baby beetroot (beets)
250 g (9 oz/1²/3 cups) fresh broad (fava) beans
200 g (7 oz) tatsoi
80 ml (2¹/2 fl oz/¹/3 cup) olive oil
1 tablespoon lemon juice
1 tablespoon wholegrain mustard
1 tablespoon honey

1 Wearing rubber gloves, trim the baby beetroot, discarding the stalks but reserving the unblemished leaves. Bring a saucepan of water to the boil. Add the beetroot and simmer, covered, for 8–10 minutes, or until tender, then drain. Ease off the skins, pat dry with paper towels and rinse. Put the beetroot in a large shallow bowl.

2 Bring a small saucepan of water to the boil. Add a large pinch of salt and the broad beans and simmer for 2–3 minutes, then drain. When cool enough to handle, slip the beans out of their skins and add to the beetroot. Add the reserved beetroot leaves and the small inner leaves of the tatsoi.

3 To make the dressing, put the olive oil and lemon juice, wholegrain mustard and honey in a small bowl and whisk well to combine. Season with salt and freshly ground black pepper to taste. Pour over the beetroot mixture and toss gently. Serve warm.

Barbecued Potato Salad with Salsa Verde Dressing

Serves 4

1 kg (2 lb 4 oz) kipfler (fingerling) potatoes, scrubbed
60 ml (2 fl oz/1/4 cup) olive oil
2 garlic cloves, crushed

DRESSING
1 tablespoon chopped oregano
1 large handful flat-leaf (Italian) parsley
80 ml (2 1/2 fl oz/1/3 cup) extra virgin olive oil
3 garlic cloves, crushed
2 tablespoons capers, drained and rinsed
2 anchovy fillets, drained
1 tablespoon lemon juice

1 Preheat a covered barbecue to medium heat. Cut the potatoes in half on the diagonal. Put in a bowl with the oil and garlic and spread them on the barbecue grill. Lower the lid and cook the potatoes for 5 minutes on each side, or until cooked through.

2 Put the dressing ingredients in a food processor and blend until smooth. Season to taste with salt and black pepper.

3 Put the potatoes in a serving bowl and toss the salsa verde through.

Roasted Carrots with Olive Oil and Garlic

Serves 4

750 g (1 lb 10 oz) carrots
1 tablespoon olive oil
3 garlic cloves, unpeeled
2 garlic cloves, sliced
2 tablespoons mascarpone cheese
2 teaspoons extra virgin olive oil
2 teaspoons lime juice
1/4 teaspoon grated lime zest

1 Preheat the oven to 220°C (425°F/Gas 7). Scrub the carrots and cut them lengthways into quarters. Put the carrots on a baking tray with the olive oil and a large pinch of salt. Toss to coat, then spread in a single layer. Roast for 30 minutes.

2 Add the unpeeled garlic cloves and the sliced garlic cloves and roast for a further 10 minutes, or until the carrots are golden and tender.

3 Squeeze the garlic from the unpeeled cloves into a small bowl and mash to a paste. Add the mascarpone cheese, extra virgin olive oil, lime juice, lime zest and salt and pepper to taste. Serve the carrots and sliced garlic with the dressing spooned over the top.

Classic Creamy Mashed Potato

Serves 4

4 large all-purpose potatoes, cut into quarters
1–2 tablespoons milk
20 g (3/4 oz) butter

1 Put the potatoes in a large saucepan of salted water and bring to the boil. Cook for 10–15 minutes, or until tender. Drain well, then return to the pan, stirring over low heat until any liquid evaporates. Mash with a potato masher until smooth.

2 Add the milk and butter, then beat into the potato with a wooden spoon. Season to taste and serve.

Asparagus Purée

Serves 4

30 g (1 oz) butter
1 tablespoon oil
3 spring onions (scallions), chopped
315 g (11 oz) young chopped asparagus, chopped
125 ml (4 fl oz/^{1}/2 cup) vegetable stock
125 ml (4 fl oz/^{1}/2 cup) pouring (whipping) cream
25 g (1 oz) grated parmesan cheese

1   Heat the butter and oil in a saucepan over medium heat. Add the
    spring onions and asparagus and cook for 3 minutes.

2   Add the vegetable stock and cream, then cover and simmer until
    tender. Remove the vegetables from the liquid and process the
    vegetables in a food processor until smooth.

3   Bring the liquid to boil and reduce by one quarter. Return the purée
    to pan. Stir in the parmesan cheese. Cook over medium heat for
    5 minutes, or until the purée thickens slightly. Season with salt and
    freshly ground black pepper.

Orange Sweet Potato Wedges with Tangy Cumin Mayonnaise

serves 4

2¹/₂ tablespoons olive oil

1 kg (2 lb 4 oz) orange sweet potato, peeled and cut into 6 cm (2¹/₂ in) long wedges

200 g (7 oz) mayonnaise

60 ml (2 fl oz/¹/₄ cup) lime juice

1 teaspoon honey

1 heaped tablespoon roughly chopped coriander (cilantro) leaves

1¹/₂ teaspoons ground cumin

1 Preheat the oven to 200°C (400°F/Gas 6). Pour the olive oil into a large roasting tin and heat in the oven for 5 minutes.

2 Place the sweet potato in the tin in a single layer, season with salt and pepper and bake for 35 minutes, turning occasionally.

3 Put the mayonnaise, lime juice, honey, coriander and cumin in a food processor and blend until smooth.

4 Drain the wedges on crumpled paper towels and serve with the tangy cumin mayonnaise on the side.

Stuffed Capsicums Grilled Tomatoes Cucumbe

Fruits and vines

And Olive Salad Spicy Eggplant Greek Salad

Fried Green Tomatoes

serves 4

125 g (4¹/2 oz/1 cup) self-raising flour
100 g (3¹/2 oz/²/3 cup) polenta
1 egg, lightly beaten
250 ml (9 fl oz/1 cup) buttermilk
6–8 green tomatoes
oil, for frying

1 Combine the flour and polenta in a bowl. Season with salt and pepper. Place the beaten egg and buttermilk in a separate bowl and whisk to combine.

2 Cut the tomatoes into 1 cm (¹/2 in) slices. Dip the tomato slices into the egg and buttermilk mixture, then toss in the flour mixture to coat. Shake off any excess flour.

3 Heat 2 cm (³/4 in) oil in a large heavy-based frying pan. Cook the tomatoes in batches over high heat until crisp and golden brown on both sides. Drain on paper towels.

 Do not overcrowd the pan, or the temperature will drop and the tomatoes will absorb the oil.

Deep-fried Zucchini Flowers

serves 4

2 eggs
60 g (2¼ oz/½ cup) plain (all-purpose) flour
10–12 zucchini (courgette) flowers

STUFFING
125 g (4½ oz) ricotta cheese
1 tablespoon chopped basil
2 tablespoons grated parmesan cheese
2 tablespoons fresh breadcrumbs
1 egg yolk

1 Whisk the eggs with the flour and season with salt and pepper.

2 To make the stuffing for the flowers, mix the ricotta with the basil,
   parmesan, breadcrumbs and egg yolk. Season well. Stuff the mixture
   into the flowers. Add a little cold water to the batter if it needs
   thinning, then dip each flower and zucchini in the batter and
   deep-fry until golden. Serve immediately.

 Before using zucchini flowers, remove and
discard the stamen from inside the flower,
wash the flower and make sure it doesn't
harbour any insects. They only last a few
days after being picked, so buy them on the
day you plan to use them.

Warm Pumpkin Salad with Preserved Lemon

Serves 4

1 kg (2 lb 4 oz) pumpkin (winter squash) or butternut pumpkin (squash)
1 preserved lemon
60 ml (2 fl oz/¼ cup) olive oil
1 onion, grated
½ teaspoon ground ginger
½ teaspoon ground cumin
1 teaspoon paprika
2 tablespoons chopped flat-leaf (Italian) parsley
2 tablespoons chopped coriander (cilantro) leaves
1 tablespoon lemon juice

1 Peel and remove the seeds from the pumpkin. Cut the pumpkin into 2 cm (¾ in) cubes. Remove the pulp from the preserved lemon and rinse and dice the rind.

2 Heat the olive oil in a large lidded frying pan. Add the onion and cook over medium heat for 3 minutes. Stir in the ginger, cumin and paprika and cook for a further 30 seconds. Add the pumpkin, parsley and coriander leaves, lemon juice, the preserved lemon rind and 125 ml (4 fl oz/½ cup) water. Season, cover and simmer over low heat for 20 minutes, or until tender, tossing occasionally and adding a little more water if necessary. Serve hot.

Eggplant Purée

Serves 6–8

2–3 eggplants (aubergines)
juice of 1 lemon
1 tablespoon oil
2 garlic cloves, crushed
125 g (4^1/$_2$ oz/^{1}/$_2$ cup) cream cheese
2 tablespoons plain yoghurt

1. Put the eggplants on a baking tray and cook for 1 hour in the oven at 180°C (350°F/Gas 4).

2. Cut in half, scoop out the pulp and purée in a blender or food processor. Add the lemon juice, oil, garlic, cream cheese and yoghurt. Blend until smooth.

3. Put in a bowl and chill for several hours before serving.

Stuffed Capsicums

Serves 6

400 g (14 oz) all-purpose potatoes, quartered

6 small green capsicums (peppers)

2 tablespoons oil

2 onions, finely chopped

2 teaspoons ground cumin

2 teaspoons ground coriander

1/2 teaspoon ground turmeric

1/2 teaspoon chilli powder

SAUCE

1/2 onion, finely chopped

6 cloves

6 cardamom pods, crushed

2 garlic cloves, finely chopped

2 cm (3/4 in) piece of ginger, finely chopped

1 cinnamon stick

1 teaspoon ground coriander

1 teaspoon ground cumin

1/4 teaspoon ground turmeric

1/2 teaspoon chilli powder

250 ml (9 fl oz/1 cup) coconut cream

1 Cook the potato in a saucepan of simmering water for 15 minutes, or until tender, then drain and cut into small cubes. Bring a large saucepan of water to the boil, add the capsicum and blanch for 5 minutes. Refresh the capsicum in cold water, cut around the stem and remove both it and the seeds. Drain well upside down.

2 Heat the oil in a small frying pan and cook the onion over medium heat until soft but not browned. Add the cumin, coriander, turmeric and chilli and mix well. Mix in the potato and season with salt, to taste. Remove from the heat and allow to cool. Divide into six portions and fill each capsicum with one portion.

3 To make the sauce, combine all the sauce ingredients in a deep, heavy-based frying pan and bring slowly to the boil. Reduce the heat to low, cover and simmer for 20 minutes. Season with salt to taste. Add the stuffed capsicums to the pan, arranging them so that they stand upright in a single layer, and cook for a further 5 minutes, or until the sauce is thick. Serve the capsicums with a little sauce spooned over the top.

Choose capsicums that are free of wrinkles or soft spots, and store in the refrigerator crisper for up to 1 week. Cut capsicums should be wrapped in paper rather than plastic, which will make them sweat and perish.

Zucchini with Mint and Feta

Serves 4

6 zucchini (courgettes)
1 tablespoon olive oil
70 g (2$^1/_2$ oz/$^1/_2$ cup) crumbled feta cheese
1 teaspoon finely grated lemon zest
$^1/_2$ teaspoon chopped garlic
1 tablespoon lemon juice
1 tablespoon extra virgin olive oil
2 tablespoons shredded mint
2 tablespoons shredded flat-leaf (Italian) parsley

1 Slice each zucchini lengthways into four thick batons. Heat the olive oil in a heavy-based, non-stick frying pan and cook the zucchini over medium heat for 3–4 minutes, or until just tender and lightly golden. Arrange on a serving plate.

2 Crumble the feta over the zucchini. Mix the lemon zest, garlic and lemon juice in a small bowl. Whisk in the extra virgin olive oil with a fork until well combined, then pour the dressing over the zucchini. Top with the mint and parsley, and season with salt and pepper. Serve warm.

 When shopping, look for firm, unblemished zucchini. Eat as soon as possible after purchase, as refrigeration makes the texture deteriorate. There is no need to peel them; in fact, most of the flavour is in the skin.

Chargrilled Eggplant Salad

Serves 4

2 large eggplants (aubergines), thinly sliced lengthways
2 garlic cloves, crushed
150 ml (5 fl oz) extra virgin olive oil
juice of 1 small lemon
$1/2$ red chilli, finely chopped
1 large handful basil or mint leaves, roughly chopped

1   Heat a chargrill pan over high heat and cook the eggplant, a few
    slices at a time, until soft and cooked. As you remove the eggplant
    slices from the pan, put them on a plate on top of each other—this
    helps them to steam a little and soften further.

2   Mix together the garlic, olive oil, lemon juice, chilli and herbs. Put
    the eggplant in a flat dish and pour over the marinade. Mix briefly
    without breaking up the eggplant and marinate for at least
    30 minutes before serving.

Pumpkin and Cashew Stir-Fry

serves 4–6

oil, for cooking
155 g (5 oz/1 cup) raw cashews
1 leek, trimmed and sliced
2 teaspoons ground coriander
2 teaspoons ground cumin
2 teaspoons brown mustard seeds
2 garlic cloves, crushed
1 kg (2 lb 4 oz) butternut pumpkin (squash), cubed
185 ml (6 fl oz/3/4 cup) orange juice
1 teaspoon soft brown sugar

1   Heat a wok until very hot, add 1 tablespoon of the oil and swirl
    to coat. Stir-fry the cashews until golden, then drain on paper
    towels. Stir-fry the leek for 2–3 minutes, or until softened. Remove
    from the wok.

2   Reheat the wok, add 1 tablespoon of the oil and stir-fry the
    coriander, cumin, mustard seeds and garlic for 2 minutes, or until
    the spices are fragrant and the mustard seeds begin to pop. Add
    the pumpkin and stir to coat well. Stir-fry for 5 minutes, or until the
    pumpkin is brown and tender.

3   Add the orange juice and sugar. Bring to the boil and cook for
    5 minutes. Add the leek and three-quarters of the cashews and
    toss well. Top with the remaining cashews.

Sichuan-style Spicy Eggplant

serves 6

500 g (1 lb 2 oz) Chinese eggplants (aubergines) or
thin eggplants (aubergines)
1/2 teaspoon salt
60 ml (2 fl oz/1/4 cup) light soy sauce
1 tablespoons Chinese rice wine
1 tablespoon roasted sesame oil
2 teaspoons clear rice vinegar
1 teaspoon soft brown sugar
1 spring onion (scallions), finely chopped
2 garlic cloves, finely chopped
1 teaspoon chilli bean paste (toban jiang)

1 Peel the eggplants and trim off the ends. Cut the eggplants in half lengthways and cut each half into strips 2 cm (3/4 in) thick. Cut the strips into 5 cm (2 in) lengths. Place the eggplant in a bowl, add the salt and toss lightly, then set aside for 1 hour. Pour off any water that has accumulated.

2 Arrange the eggplant on a heatproof plate and place in a steamer. Cover and steam over simmering water in a wok for 20 minutes, or until tender. Combine the remaining ingredients in a bowl, then pour the sauce over the eggplant, tossing lightly to coat.

Cucumber, Feta, Mint and Dill Salad

Serves 4

120 g (4 oz) feta cheese
4 Lebanese (short) cucumbers
1 small red onion, thinly sliced
1¹/2 tablespoons finely chopped dill
1 tablespoon dried mint
60 ml (2 fl oz/¹/4 cup) olive oil
1¹/2 tablespoons lemon juice

1 Crumble the feta into 1 cm (¹/2 in) pieces and place in a large bowl. Peel and seed the cucumbers and cut into 1 cm (¹/2 in) dice. Add to the bowl along with the onion and dill.

2 Grind the mint in a mortar and pestle, or force through a sieve, until powdered. Combine with the oil and lemon juice, then season with salt and black pepper. Pour over the salad and toss well.

Roasted Red Capsicums

serves 4-6

8 red capsicums (peppers)
2 garlic cloves, crushed
80 ml (2³/4 fl oz/¹/3 cup) red wine vinegar
2 teaspoons thyme

1 Cut the capsicums into four flattish pieces each and carefully remove the seeds and membranes. Arrange in a single layer on a baking tray and cook under a hot grill (broiler) until the skins are blackened and blistered.

2 Put the capsicum in a large bowl, then cover with plastic wrap and set aside for 10 minutes. Peel away the skins and slice the flesh into 3 cm (1¹/4 in) wide strips. Put the strips in a clean bowl.

3 Combine the garlic and red wine vinegar in a small bowl and season with salt. Pour the dressing over the capsicum and gently toss to coat. Sprinkle thyme leaves over the top and refrigerate for at least 4 hours before serving.

Tunisian Eggplant Salad with Preserved Lemon

serves 4

2 large eggplants (aubergines)

1–2 teaspoons salt

125 ml (4 fl oz/$1/2$ cup) olive oil, plus extra to serve

1 teaspoon cumin seeds

2 garlic cloves, very thinly sliced

1 tablespoon currants

1 tablespoon slivered almonds

6 small roma (plum) tomatoes, quartered lengthways

1 teaspoon dried oregano

$1/2$ preserved lemon

4 red bird's eye chillies, halved lengthways and seeded

2 tablespoons lemon juice

1 handful chopped flat-leaf (Italian) parsley

1 Cut the eggplants into 2 cm ($3/4$ in) cubes, put in a large colander and sprinkle with the salt. Set aside to drain in the sink for 2–3 hours. Dry with paper towels.

2 Heat half the olive oil in a large flameproof casserole dish over medium–high heat. Fry the eggplant in batches for 5–6 minutes, or until golden, adding more oil as required. Drain on paper towels.

3 Reduce the heat and add any remaining oil to the casserole dish, along with the cumin, garlic, currants and almonds. Fry for 20–30 seconds, or until the garlic starts to colour. Add the tomato and oregano and cook for 1 minute. Remove from the heat.

4   Trim the rind from the piece of preserved lemon and cut the rind into thin strips. Discard the flesh.

5   Return the eggplant to the casserole and add the chilli, lemon juice, parsley and preserved lemon zest. Toss gently and season with freshly ground black pepper. Set aside at room temperature for at least 1 hour before serving. Check the seasoning, then drizzle with extra virgin olive oil.

Eggplant comes in many shapes and colours, but the one that is favoured for grilling is the handsome egg-shaped purple variety. Look for a smooth skin without dimples, a uniformly firm flesh, a bright-green stem base and an obvious ridge running down one side.

Zucchini Wrapped in Prosciutto

Serves 4

2 small green zucchini (courgettes)
2 small yellow zucchini (courgettes)
8 thin slices prosciutto

SAGE BUTTER
40 g (1 1/2 oz) butter, softened
1 tablespoon finely chopped sage
1 tablespoon finely chopped semi-dried (sun-blushed) tomatoes

1 Preheat a barbecue flat plate to low. Bring a large saucepan of water to the boil. Add the whole zucchini, then reduce the heat and simmer for 5 minutes, or until almost tender. Drain well, allow to cool, then pat dry with paper towels.

2 To make the sage butter, put the butter, sage and tomato in a small bowl and mix well. Season to taste with salt and pepper and set aside.

3 Wrap 2 slices of prosciutto around each zucchini — it should stick together quite easily. Put the zucchini on the hot plate and cook for about 15 minutes, or until cooked through, turning halfway through cooking. Serve hot, with a dollop of sage butter.

Baked Capsicums with Anchovies

Serves 6

3 yellow capsicums (peppers)
3 red capsicums (peppers)
2 tablespoons extra virgin olive oil
6–12 anchovy fillets, halved lengthways
3 garlic cloves, thinly sliced
25 g (1 oz) basil
1 tablespoon baby capers, rinsed and drained
extra virgin olive oil, to serve

1   Preheat the oven to 180°C (350°F/Gas 4). Cut each capsicum in half lengthways, leaving the stems intact. If the capsicums are large, quarter them. Remove the seeds and membrane. Drizzle a little of the oil in a baking dish and place the capsicum halves in, skin side down. Season with salt and pepper.

2   In each capsicum, place a halved anchovy fillet, slivers of garlic and a torn basil leaf. Divide the capers among the capsicum pieces. Season with salt and pepper and drizzle with the remaining oil.

3   Cover the dish with foil and bake the capsicum for 20 minutes. Remove the foil and cook for a further 25–30 minutes, or until the capsicum are tender. Drizzle with a little extra virgin olive oil. Scatter the remaining torn basil leaves over the capsicum and serve warm or at room temperature.

Avocado and Black Bean Salad

Serves 4

250 g (9 oz) dried black beans
1 red onion, chopped
4 roma (plum) tomatoes, chopped
1 red capsicum (pepper), chopped
375 g (13 oz) canned corn kernels, drained
90 g (3¼ oz) coriander (cilantro), roughly chopped
2 avocados, peeled and chopped
1 mango, peeled and chopped
150 g (5½ oz) rocket, leaves separated

DRESSING
1 garlic clove, crushed
1 small red chilli, finely chopped
2 tablespoons lime juice
60 ml (2 fl oz/¼ cup) olive oil

1 Soak the beans in cold water overnight. Rinse thoroughly, then drain. Place the beans into a large heavy-based saucepan, cover with water and bring to the boil. Reduce the heat and simmer for 1½ hours, or until tender. Drain and allow to cool slightly.

2 Place the beans, onion, tomatoes, capsicum, corn, coriander, avocado, mango and rocket into a large bowl and toss to combine.

3 To make the dressing, put all the ingredients in a bowl and whisk to combine. Pour over the salad and toss well.

Zucchini, Radish and Feta Salad

Serves 4

DRESSING
1 tablespoon white wine vinegar
2 tablespoons olive oil
2–3 teaspoons wholegrain mustard

5 small zucchini (courgettes)
2 teaspoons salt
6 radishes, thinly sliced
1/2 small red onion, thinly sliced
1 small cos (romaine) lettuce
100 g (31/2 oz/2/3 cup) feta cheese

1 To make the dressing, combine the white wine vinegar, olive oil, wholegrain mustard and salt and freshly ground black pepper.

2 Finely shave the zucchini from top to bottom. Place in a colander, sprinkle with salt and set aside to drain in the sink for 30 minutes. Do not rinse. Gently dry with paper towels and put in a large bowl.

3 Add the radishes and red onion to the bowl. Tear the inner leaves of the cos lettuce into smaller pieces and add to the bowl. Add the dressing and toss lightly. Transfer to a shallow serving dish and crumble the feta cheese over the top before serving.

Greek Salad

Serves 4

1 large tomato, cut into wedges
1 Lebanese (short) cucumber, sliced
2 radishes, thinly sliced
1 small onion, thinly sliced
100 g (3$^1/_3$ oz) feta cheese, cut into small cubes
45 g (1$^1/_2$ oz/$^1/_4$ cup) pitted black olives
2 tablespoons lemon juice
60 ml (2 fl oz/$^1/_4$ cup) olive oil
$^1/_2$ teaspoon dried oregano

1 Combine the tomato, cucumber, radish, onion, feta and olives in a serving bowl. Drizzle with the combined lemon juice and olive oil, then top with the oregano leaves.

When buying cucumbers, choose firm ones with no signs of bruising and store them in the refrigerator wrapped in plastic to prevent their odour spreading to other foods.

Roast Tomato Salad

Serves 6

6 roma (plum) tomatoes
2 teaspoons capers, rinsed and drained
6 basil leaves, torn
1 tablespoon olive oil
1 tablespoon balsamic vinegar
2 garlic cloves, crushed
1/2 teaspoon honey

1　Cut the tomatoes lengthways into quarters. Place on a baking tray, skin side down, and cook under a hot grill (broiler) for 4–5 minutes, or until golden. Cool to room temperature and put in a bowl.

2　Combine the capers, basil leaves, olive oil, balsamic vinegar, crushed garlic and honey in a bowl, season with salt and freshly ground black pepper, and pour over the tomatoes. Gently toss to combine.

Spicy Eggplant

Serves 6

800 g (1 lb 12 oz) eggplant (aubergine), cut into wedges 5 cm (2 in) long
400 g (14 oz) ripe tomatoes
2.5 cm (1 in) piece of ginger, grated
6 garlic cloves, crushed
300 ml (10^1/$_2$ fl oz) oil
1 teaspoon fennel seeds
^{1}/$_2$ teaspoon nigella seeds
1 tablespoon ground coriander
^{1}/$_4$ teaspoon ground turmeric
^{1}/$_2$ teaspoon cayenne pepper
1 teaspoon salt

1 Put the eggplant pieces in a colander, sprinkle with salt and leave for 30 minutes to allow any bitter juices to run out. Rinse, squeeze out any excess water, then pat dry with paper towels.

2 Score a cross in the top of each tomato and plunge into boiling water for 20 seconds. Drain and peel away from the cross. Chop the tomatoes, discarding the cores and seeds and reserving any juices.

3 Purée the ginger and garlic with one-third of the tomato in a blender or food processor.

4 Heat 125 ml (4 fl oz/^{1}/$_2$ cup) of the oil in a deep, heavy-based frying pan and when hot, add as many eggplant pieces as you can fit in a single layer. Cook over medium heat until brown on both sides, then transfer to a sieve over a bowl so that the excess oil can drain off. Add the remaining oil to the pan as needed and cook the remaining eggplant in batches.

5 Reheat the remaining oil left in the pan and add the fennel seeds and nigella seeds. Cover and allow to pop for a few seconds. Add the tomato and ginger mixture and the remaining ingredients, except the eggplant. Cook, stirring regularly for 5–6 minutes, until the mixture becomes thick and fairly smooth. Carefully add the cooked eggplant so the pieces stay whole, cover the pan and cook gently for about 10 minutes.

Store the eggplant in the sauce in the fridge. Pour off any excess oil before serving. The eggplant can either be served cold or gently warmed through.

Stuffed Zucchini Flowers

Makes 20

75 g (2¹/2 oz) plain (all-purpose) flour
100 g (3¹/2 oz) mozzarella cheese
10 basil leaves, torn
20 zucchini (courgette) flowers, stems and pistils removed
olive oil, for shallow-frying
2 lemon wedges, to serve

1 To make the batter, combine the flour with 250 ml (9 fl oz/1 cup) water in a bowl. Add a pinch of salt and mix well.

2 Cut the mozzarella cheese into 20 matchsticks. Insert a piece of mozzarella and some basil into each zucchini blossom. Gently press the petals closed.

3 Pour oil into a heavy-based frying pan to a depth of 2.5 cm (1 in). Heat until a drop of batter sizzles when dropped in the oil.

4 Dip one flower at a time in the batter, shaking off the excess. Cook in batches for 3 minutes, or until crisp and golden. Drain on paper towels. Season and serve immediately with lemon wedges.

Pumpkin with Saffron and Coriander Butter

Serves 6

SAFFRON AND CORIANDER BUTTER
small pinch of saffron threads
50 g (1³/4 oz) butter, softened
1 tablespoon finely chopped coriander (cilantro) leaves

¹/2 pumpkin (winter squash)
olive oil, for brushing
1 handful coriander (cilantro) leaves

1 To make the saffron and coriander butter, put the saffron in a small bowl, add 2 teaspoons hot water and leave to soak for at least 20 minutes. Add the butter and coriander and mix until combined. Put the butter mixture into the centre of a piece of plastic wrap, then roll up into a 7 cm (2³/4 in) log. Refrigerate for about 30 minutes, or until firm.

2 Preheat a barbecue grill plate or chargrill pan to high. Slice the unpeeled pumpkin into 2 cm (³/4 in) thick wedges and discard the seeds. Brush the wedges on both sides with oil and season with salt and freshly ground black pepper.

3 Grill the pumpkin for 10 minutes on each side, or until browned and tender. Place on a serving platter and top with the sliced saffron and coriander butter. Allow the butter to melt a little and serve the pumpkin hot, scattered with coriander leaves.

Eggplant and Lentil Salad

Serves 4–6

60 ml (2 fl oz/$1/4$ cup) olive oil
300 g ($10^{1}/_{2}$ oz) eggplant (aubergine), diced into 5 mm ($1/4$ in) cubes
1 small red onion, finely diced
$1/4$ teaspoon ground cumin
3 garlic cloves, chopped
200 g (7 oz) puy lentils
375 ml (13 fl oz/$1^{1}/_{2}$ cups) vegetable stock
2 tablespoons chopped flat-leaf (Italian) parsley
1 tablespoon red wine vinegar
1 tablespoon extra virgin olive oil

1   Heat 2 tablespoons of the olive oil in a large frying pan over medium heat. Add the eggplant and cook, stirring constantly, for 5 minutes, or until soft. Add the onion and cumin and cook for a further 2–3 minutes, or until the onion has softened. Put the mixture in a bowl and season well.

2   Heat the remaining olive oil in the frying pan over medium heat. Add the garlic and cook for 1 minute. Add the lentils and stock and cook, stirring regularly, over low heat for 40 minutes, or until the liquid has evaporated and the lentils are tender.

3   Add the lentils to the bowl with the eggplant and stir in the parsley and red wine vinegar. Season well with salt and black pepper, drizzle with the extra virgin olive oil and serve warm.

Red Capsicum Salad

Serves 4

1 kg (2 lb 4 oz) red capsicums (peppers)
3 large garlic cloves, unpeeled
1 large tomato
80 ml (2½ fl oz/⅓ cup) extra virgin olive oil
1 teaspoon sherry vinegar
1 tablespoon chopped flat-leaf (Italian) parsley

1 Preheat the oven to 200°C (400°F/Gas 6). Put the capsicums in a roasting tin and rub all over with olive oil. Add the garlic cloves and tomato and cook for 15 minutes. Remove the garlic and tomato, turn the capsicums and cook for a further 15 minutes.

2 Skin, seed and chop the tomato flesh, reserving the juice. Peel the garlic. Put the capsicum in a bag to cool, then peel, seed and slice the flesh into strips, reserving the juice.

3 Arrange the capsicum strips on a serving dish. Pound or process the garlic and tomato to a paste. Add the extra virgin olive oil, sherry vinegar and the reserved tomato and capsicum juices and mix through. Pour the dressing over the capsicum and sprinkle with the parsley.

Grilled Green Tomatoes with Walnut Crumble

Serves 4–6

4 green tomatoes

75 g (2¹/2 oz/1 cup) coarse fresh breadcrumbs, made from an Italian
bread such as ciabatta

1 garlic clove, crushed

2 tablespoons roughly chopped walnuts

40 g (1¹/2 oz) butter, melted

2 tablespoons roughly chopped flat-leaf (Italian) parsley

1 tablespoon roughly chopped oregano

2 tablespoons grated parmesan cheese

1 Heat the grill (broiler) to medium. Cut each tomato into six wedges, remove the core and sit the wedges in a shallow, lightly oiled ovenproof dish. Put the dish under the grill and cook the tomato for 5 minutes, or until heated through, turning the wedges over once during cooking.

2 Combine all the remaining ingredients in a bowl and season with salt and pepper. Sprinkle the mixture over the tomatoes and grill for a further 5–6 minutes, or until the topping is golden brown and the tomatoes are hot.

Chargrilled Eggplant with Fresh Lemon Pesto

Serves 4-6

2 large eggplants (aubergines), cut into 1.5 cm (5/8 in) slices
170 ml (5 1/2 fl oz/2/3 cup) extra virgin olive oil
60 g (2 1/4 oz/2 cups) basil leaves
20 g (3/4 oz/1 cup) flat-leaf (Italian) parsley
50 g (1 3/4 oz/1/3 cup) pine nuts, roasted
1 1/2 garlic cloves
60 g (2 1/4 oz) grated parmesan cheese
grated zest of 1 lemon
60 ml (2 fl oz/1/4 cup) lemon juice

1 Brush both sides of the eggplant slices with 2 tablespoons of the extra virgin olive oil. Heat a chargrill pan until hot, and cook the eggplant slices for 3 minutes, or until golden and cooked through on both sides. Cover the eggplant to keep warm.

2 To make the pesto, put the basil, parsley, pine nuts, garlic, parmesan, lemon zest and lemon juice in a food processor, and blend together. Slowly add the remaining olive oil and process until the mixture forms a smooth paste. Season with salt and freshly ground black pepper.

3 Stack the eggplant on a platter, drizzling some pesto between each layer.

Grilled Tomatoes

Serves 4

4 large ripe tomatoes
2 garlic cloves, crushed
60 ml (2 fl oz/¼ cup) olive oil
1 tablespoon chopped flat-leaf (Italian) parsley

1 Cut the tomatoes in half horizontally. Put on a baking tray, skin side up, and grill (broil) for 2 minutes, then turn.

2 Mix together the garlic, olive oil and parsley and drizzle over the tomatoes. Season with salt and pepper.

3 Put the tomatoes back under the grill and cook for 6 minutes, or until cooked. Serve hot or warm.

To improve the flavour of tomatoes, let them ripen at room temperature. Tomatoes will not ripen if left in the refrigerator.

Marinated Red Capsicums

Serves 6

3 red capsicums (peppers)
3 thyme sprigs
1 garlic clove, thinly sliced
2 teaspoons roughly chopped flat-leaf (Italian) parsley
1 bay leaf
1 spring onion (scallion), sliced
1 teaspoon sweet paprika
60 ml (2 fl oz/¼ cup) extra virgin olive oil
2 tablespoons red wine vinegar

1 Preheat the grill (broiler). Cut the capsicums into quarters, remove the seeds and membrane and grill (broil), skin side up, until the skin blackens and blisters. Cool in a plastic bag, then peel.

2 Thinly slice the capsicum, then put in a bowl with the thyme sprigs, garlic, parsley, bay leaf and spring onion. Mix well.

3 Whisk together the paprika, extra virgin olive oil, red wine vinegar and some salt and freshly ground black pepper.

4 Pour over the capsicum mixture and toss to combine. Cover and refrigerate for at least 3 hours, or preferably overnight. Remove from the refrigerator 30 minutes before serving.

Feta-filled Zucchini

Serves 6

6 zucchini (courgettes)
250 g (9 oz) feta cheese, crumbled
2 tablespoons snipped chives
1 garlic clove, crushed
2$^{1}/_{2}$ tablespoons olive oil
6 lemon wedges

1   Put the whole zucchini in a saucepan of salted, boiling water and cook for about 6 minutes, or until just tender. Drain and allow to cool slightly.

2   Heat the grill (broiler) to high. Put the feta, chives and garlic in a small bowl with 1 tablespoon of the oil and freshly ground black pepper. Mix well.

3   When the zucchini are cool enough to handle, slice a strip about 5 mm ($^{1}/_{4}$ in) deep from along the length of each zucchini and discard. Use a teaspoon to scoop out most of the seeds, and sit the zucchini cut-side-up on a lightly oiled baking tray.

4   Spoon equal amounts of the feta mixture into the cavity of each zucchini. Lightly brush each zucchini with a little of the oil and grill for about 10 minutes, or until lightly browned. Drizzle with the remaining oil, sprinkle with freshly ground black pepper and serve with the lemon wedges.

Baked Eggplant and Tomatoes

Serves 6

2 eggplants (aubergines), thinly sliced
1 tablespoon salt
5 tomatoes, sliced
1 small handful flat-leaf (Italian) parsley
2 garlic cloves, finely chopped
125 ml (4 fl oz/$\frac{1}{2}$ cup) chicken or beef stock
35 g (1$\frac{1}{4}$ oz/$\frac{1}{3}$ cup) grated parmesan cheese

1 Put the eggplant in a colander and sprinkle with salt. Allow to stand for 30–40 minutes. Drain well and pat dry with paper towels.

2 Preheat the oven to 200°C (400°F/Gas 6). Alternate layers of eggplant, tomato and parsley in overlapping rows in a lightly greased shallow baking dish. Sprinkle the garlic between the layers. Season to taste.

3 Pour the stock over. Sprinkle with the parmesan cheese. Cover and bake for 30 minutes.

4 Uncover and continue baking for a further 20 minutes, or until browned, basting with the baking juices.

If the mixture appears too dry during baking, add a little more stock as needed.

Insalata Caprese

Serves 4

6 ripe roma (plum) tomatoes
3–4 balls mozzarella cheese
2 tablespoons extra virgin olive oil
15 basil leaves
$1/2$ teaspoon balsamic vinegar (optional)

1   Slice the tomatoes, pouring off any excess juice, and cut the mozzarella into slices of a similar thickness.

2   Arrange alternating rows of tomato and mozzarella on a serving plate. Sprinkle with salt and pepper and drizzle the olive oil over the top. Tear the basil leaves into pieces and scatter over the oil. To serve, sprinkle with the balsamic vinegar, if you like.

Semi-Dried Tomatoes

Fills a 500 ml (16 fl oz) jar

16 roma (plum) tomatoes
1 teaspoon salt
1 teaspoon cracked black pepper
1 small handful thyme, chopped
2 tablespoons olive oil

1 Preheat the oven to 160°C (315°F/Gas 2–3). Cut the tomatoes into quarters lengthways and lay them, skin side down, on a wire rack in a baking tray. Sprinkle with the salt, pepper and thyme and cook in the oven for 2½ hours.

2 Toss the tomatoes in the olive oil and allow to cool before packing into sterilised jars and sealing. Store in the refrigerator for 24 hours before using.

To sterilize a storage jar, rinse with boiling water, then place in a warm oven until completely dry. Do not dry with a tea towel (dish towel). Semi-dried tomatoes should be eaten within 3–4 days.

Tabbouleh

Serves 6

130 g (4³/4 oz/³/4 cup) burghul (bulgur)
3 ripe tomatoes
1 telegraph (long) cucumber
4 spring onions (scallions), sliced
4 large handfuls chopped flat-leaf (Italian) parsley
1 handful chopped mint

DRESSING
80 ml (2¹/2 fl oz/¹/3 cup) lemon juice
1¹/2 teaspoons salt
60 ml (2 fl oz/¹/4 cup) olive oil
1 tablespoon extra virgin olive oil

1   Put the burghul in a bowl, cover with 500 ml (17 fl oz/2 cups) water and leave for 1¹/2 hours.

2   Cut the tomatoes in half, squeeze to remove any excess seeds and cut into 1 cm (¹/2 in) cubes. Cut the cucumber in half lengthways, remove the seeds with a teaspoon and cut the flesh into 1 cm (¹/2 in) cubes.

3   To make the dressing, put the lemon juice and salt in a bowl and whisk until well combined. Season with freshly ground black pepper and whisk in the olive oil and extra virgin olive oil.

4   Drain the burghul and squeeze out any excess water. Spread the burghul out on paper towels and allow to dry. Put the burghul in a bowl, add the tomato, cucumber, spring onion, parsley and mint, and toss well. Pour the dressing over the salad and toss until well coated.

Cucumber and Olive Salad

Serves 4

4 Lebanese (short) cucumbers
1/2 teaspoon salt
1 red onion, finely chopped
3 teaspoons caster (superfine) sugar
1 tablespoon red wine vinegar
60 ml (2 fl oz/1/4 cup) olive oil
1 teaspoon finely chopped lemon thyme
90 g (31/4 oz/1/2 cup) black olives

1 Wash the cucumbers and dry with paper towels. Do not peel the cucumbers if the skin is tender. Coarsely grate the cucumbers, mix with the salt and leave to drain well.

2 Add the onion and the sugar to the cucumber and toss together.

3 Beat the vinegar with the olive oil in a small bowl. Add the lemon thyme and freshly ground black pepper. Whisk the ingredients together and pour over the cucumber. Cover and chill for 15 minutes. Scatter with the olives.

Eggplant, Tahini and Mint Salad

Serves 4

DRESSING
60 g (2 1/4 oz/ 1/4 cup) tahini
2 teaspoons olive oil
1 garlic clove, crushed
2 tablespoons lemon juice

1 large eggplant (aubergine), thinly sliced
2 tablespoons olive oil
1 garlic clove, crushed
1 large handful mint, roughly chopped
1 handful chopped flat-leaf (Italian) parsley
2 tablespoons Greek-style yoghurt
1/4 teaspoon mild smoked paprika

1 Put all the tahini dressing ingredients in a food processor with
125 ml (4 fl oz/ 1/2 cup) warm water. Blend until well combined
and set aside.

2 Preheat a barbecue grill plate or chargrill pan to medium. Put the
eggplant slices in a large bowl, add the oil and garlic, then toss well
to coat. Cook the eggplant for about 3 minutes, or until grill marks
appear, turning once. Place in a large bowl and allow to cool.

3 Toss the mint, parsley and tahini dressing through the eggplant slices,
mixing well. Serve at room temperature, dolloped with yoghurt and
sprinkled with the paprika.

Avocado with Lime and Chillies

Serves 6

1 teaspoon finely grated lime rind

2 tablespoons lime juice

1 teaspoon soft brown sugar

1 tablespoon olive oil

1 tablespoon chopped fresh parsley

2–3 jalapeño chillies, seeded and diced

2 ripe avocados, peeled and sliced

1 Thoroughly combine lime rind and juice, sugar, oil, parsley and chillies in a small bowl. Pour over the sliced avocado and serve.

The lime juice prevents the avocados browning. Lemon juice may be substituted.

index